marques vickers

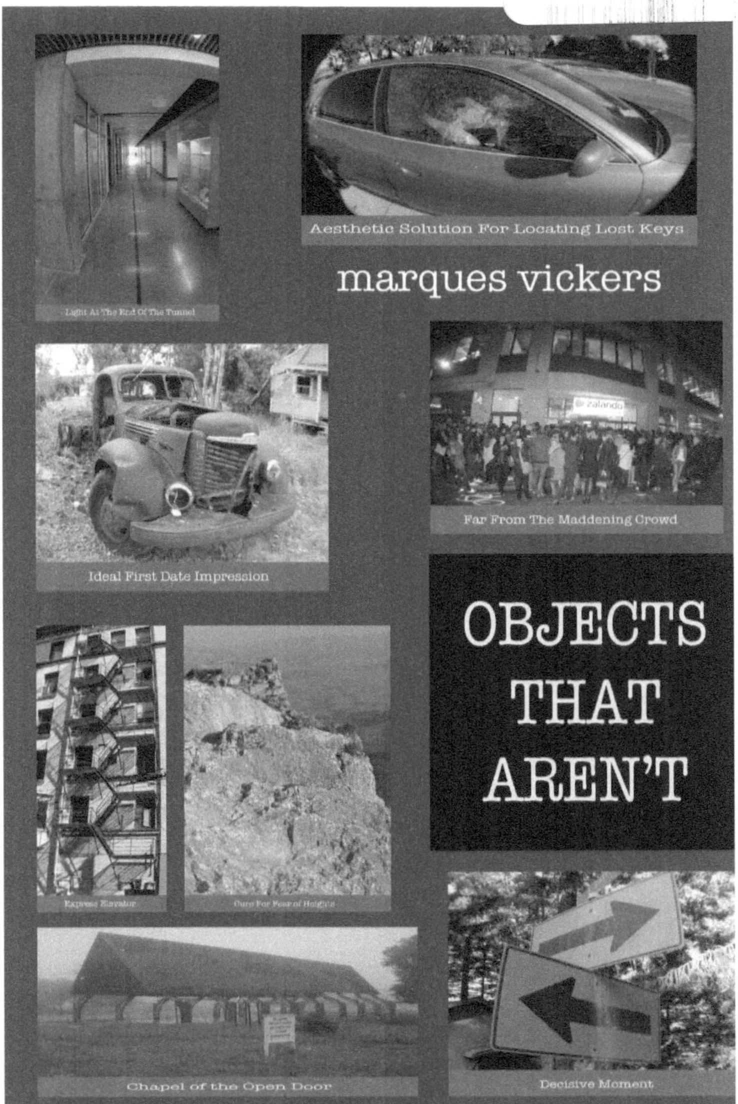

OBJECTS THAT AREN'T

OBJECTS THAT AREN'T

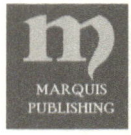

By Marques Vickers

**MARQUIS PUBLISHING
HERRON ISLAND, WASHINGTON**

@2017 Marques Vickers

All rights reserved. Copyright under Berne Copyright Convention, Universal Copyright Convention, and Pan-American Copyright Convention. No part of this book may be reproduced, stored in a retrieval system, or transmitted in any form, or by any means, electronic, mechanical, photocopying, recording, or otherwise, without prior permission of the author or publisher.

Version 1

Published by Marquis Publishing
Herron Island, Washington

Objects That Aren't

Vickers, Marques, 1957

Dedicated to my daughters Charline and Caroline

Objects That Aren't

The context of any image may entirely change based upon the perspective from which it is viewed and described. The absurd becomes probable. The exaggerated becomes envisioned. Visual reference points become distorted.

An alternative-viewing angle may completely alter the intent of an impression and its accepted interpretation.

Amidst our casual, concrete interpretations, and profound certainties towards meaning, an equally compelling argument exists to the contrary. This reinvention of meaning, dreams and definition became the foundation of the original Surrealist movement.

I may inform you of what something means (at least to me), but you not obliged to accept my interpretation.

A warped and misshapen vision lens may create an illusion far different from the one intended by the capturing photographer. This margin of difference enables an artist to label and define their unique universe.

To embrace such enlightenment may exact a price. You may be obligated to cultivate a sense of humor and suspend your well-entrenched foundation of assumptions.

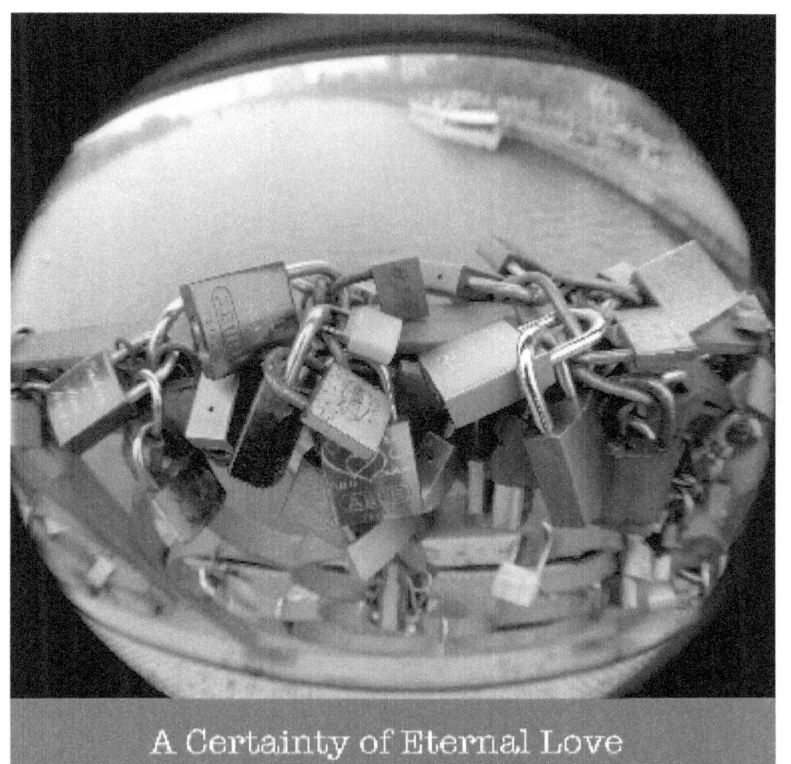

A Certainty of Eternal Love

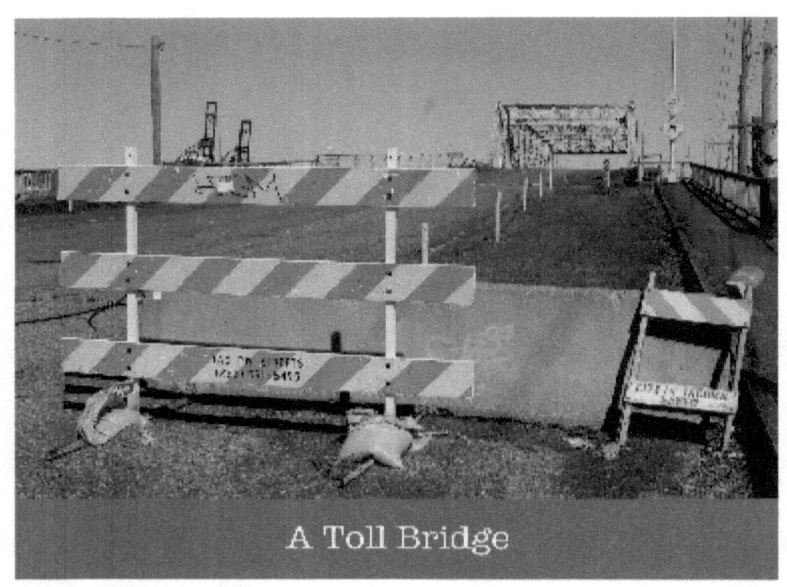

A Toll Bridge

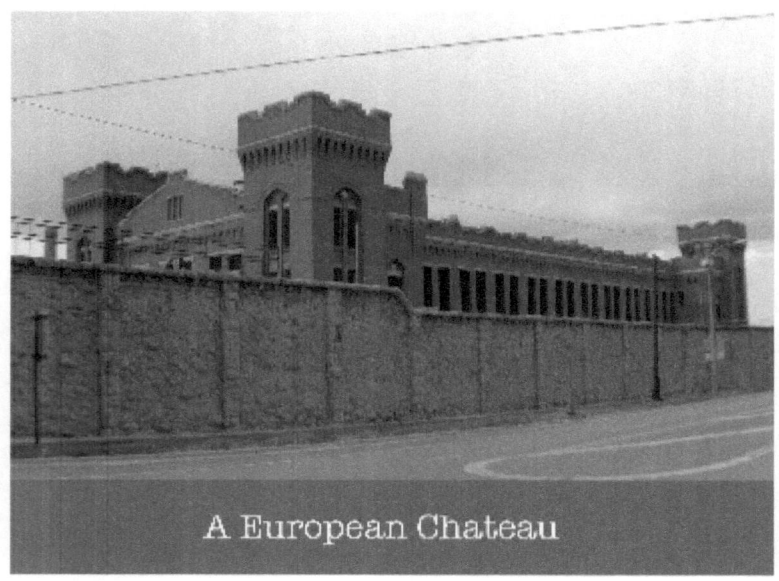

A European Chateau

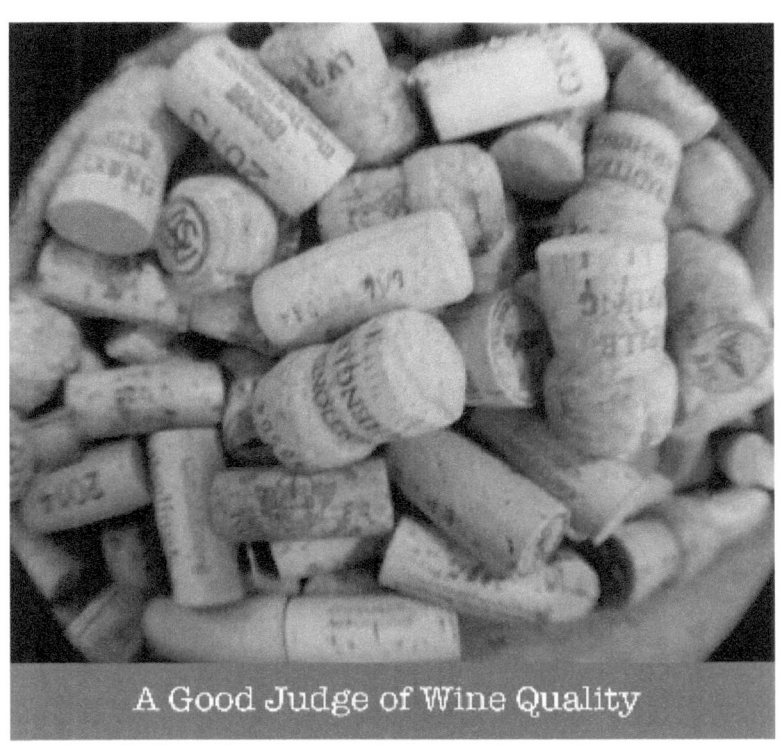
A Good Judge of Wine Quality

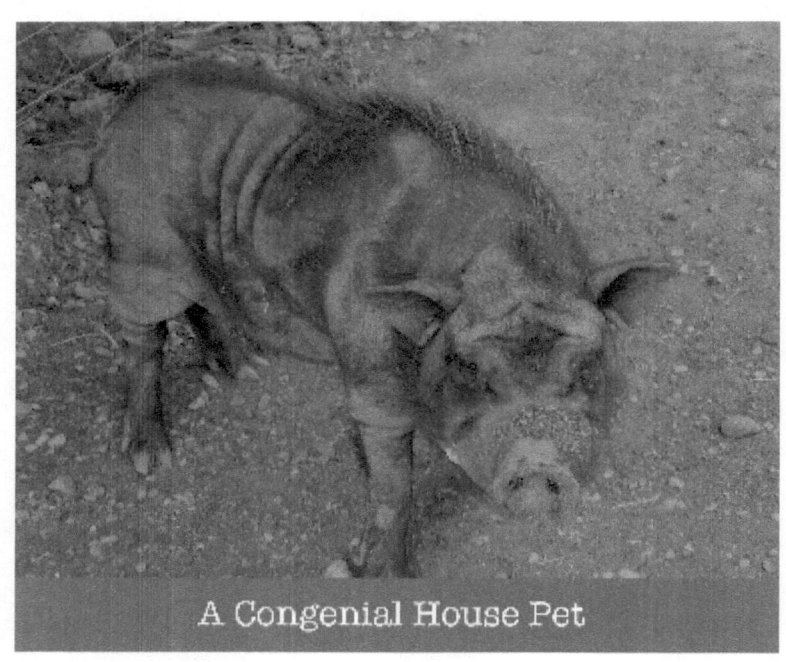
A Congenial House Pet

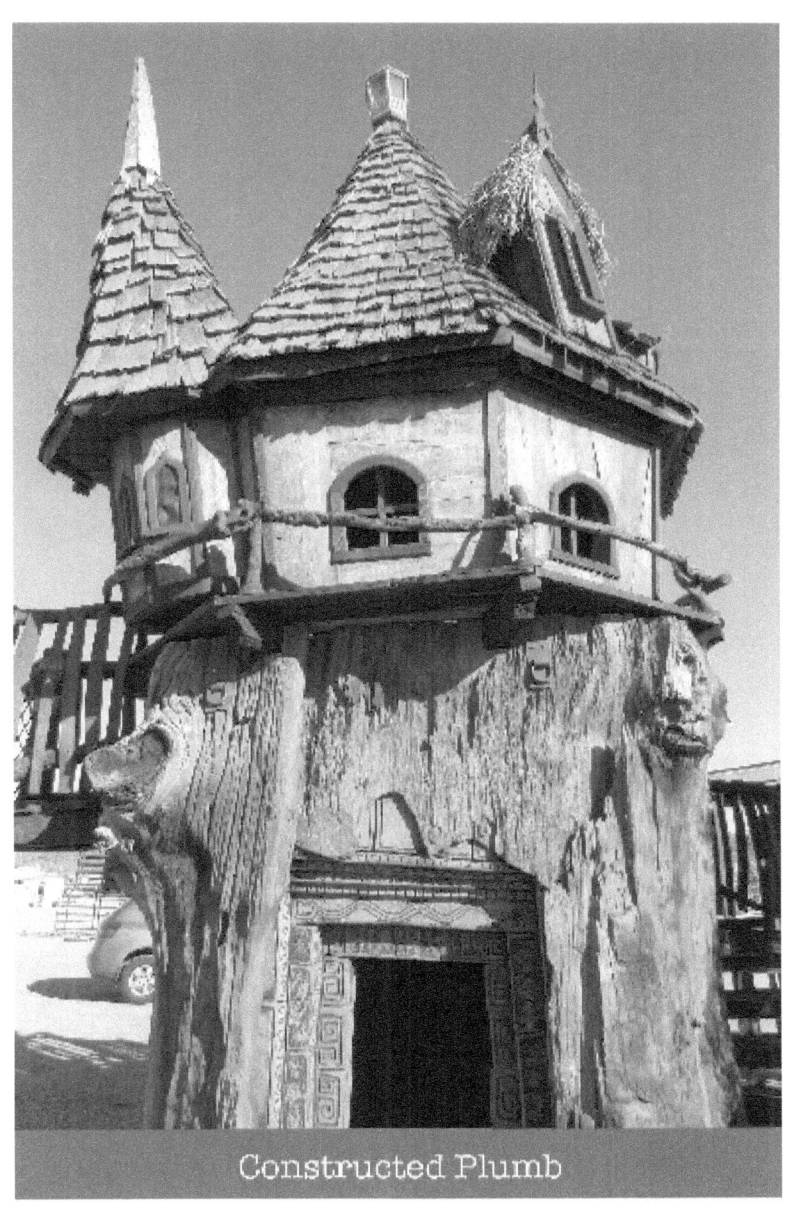
Constructed Plumb

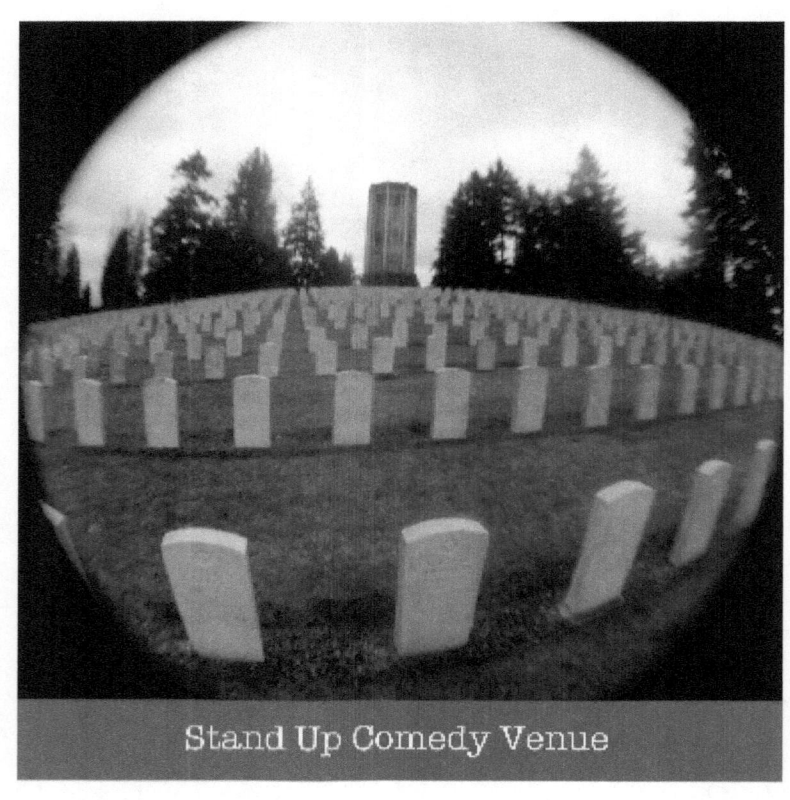

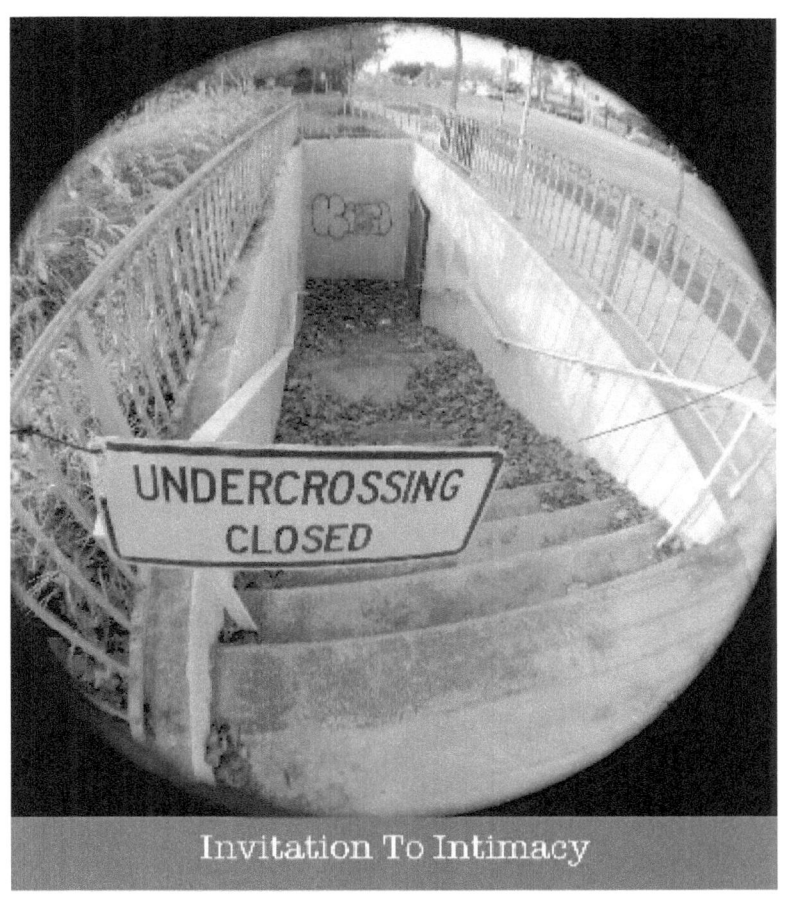

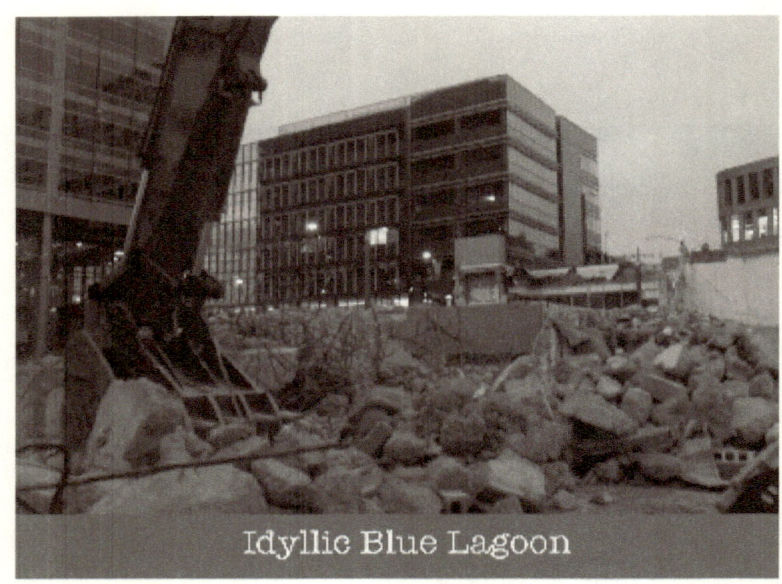

Idyllic Blue Lagoon

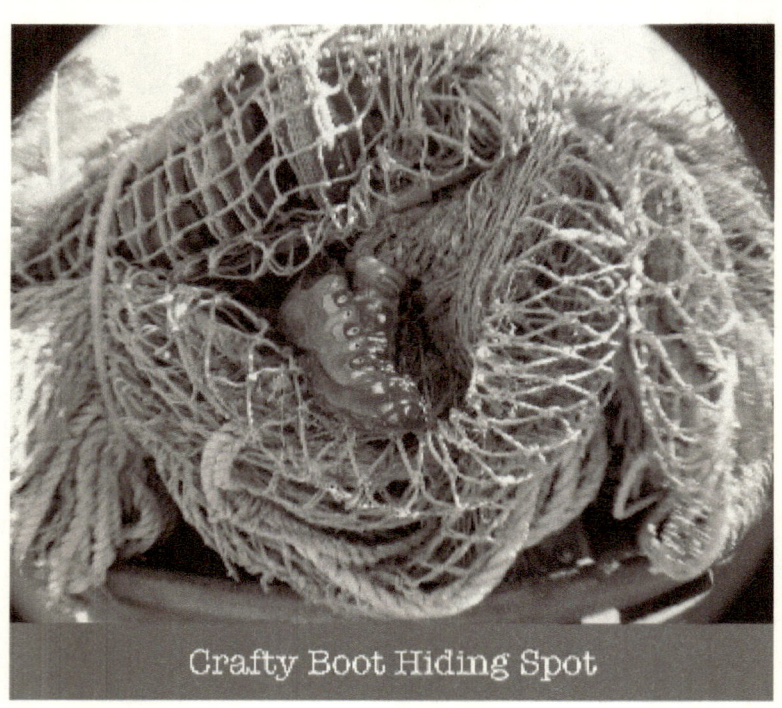

Crafty Boot Hiding Spot

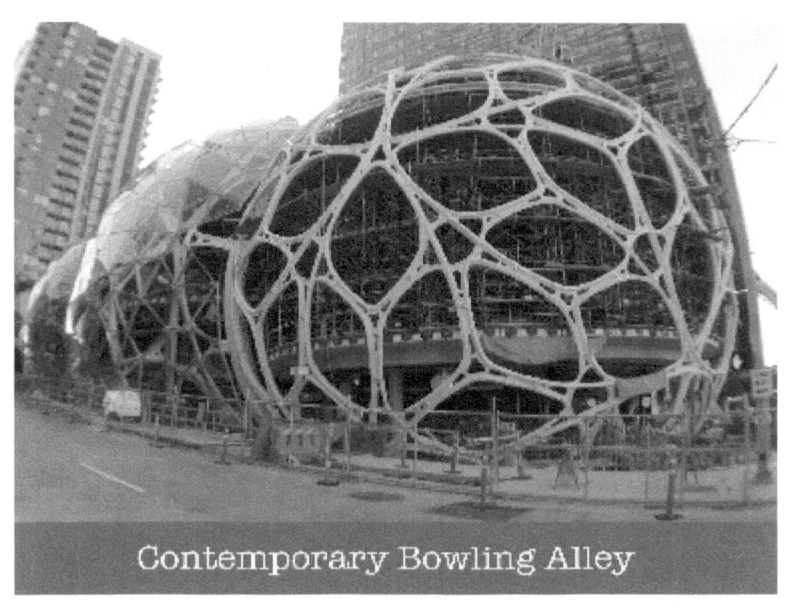
Contemporary Bowling Alley

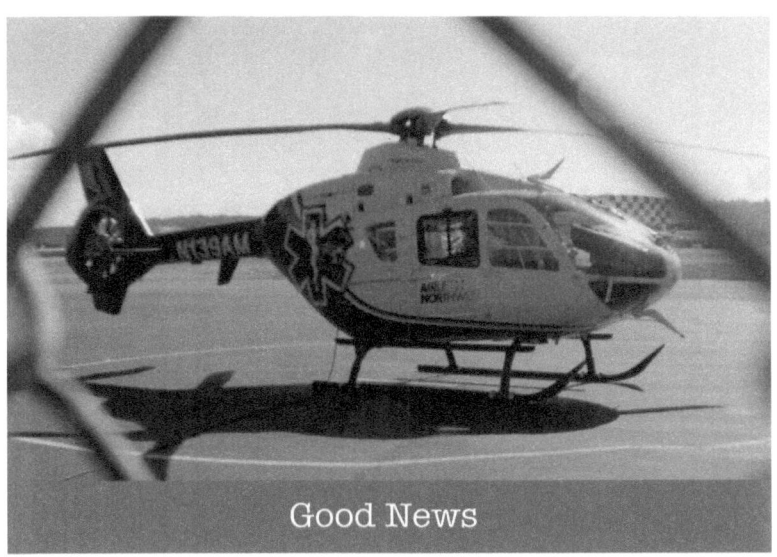
Good News

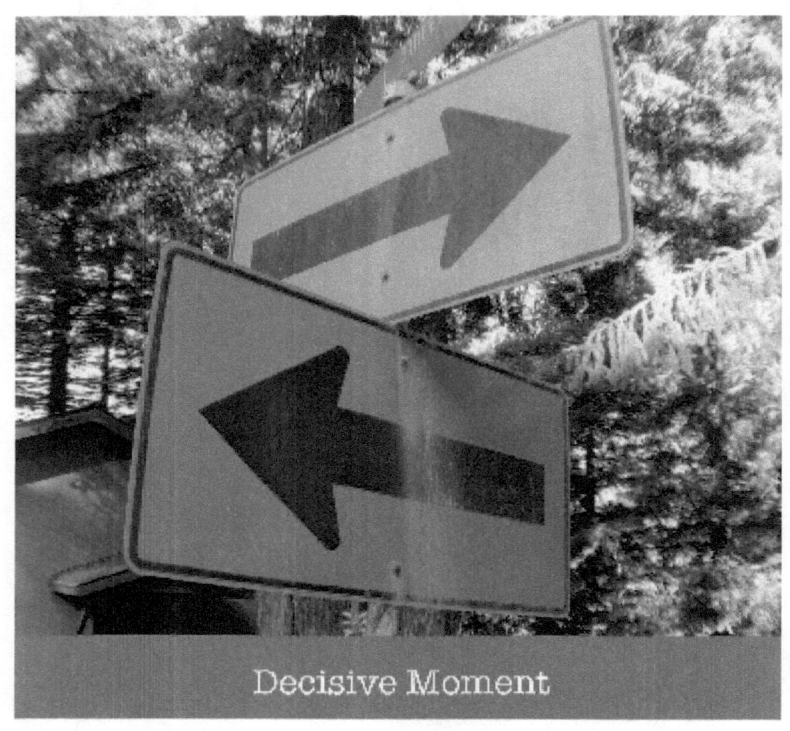

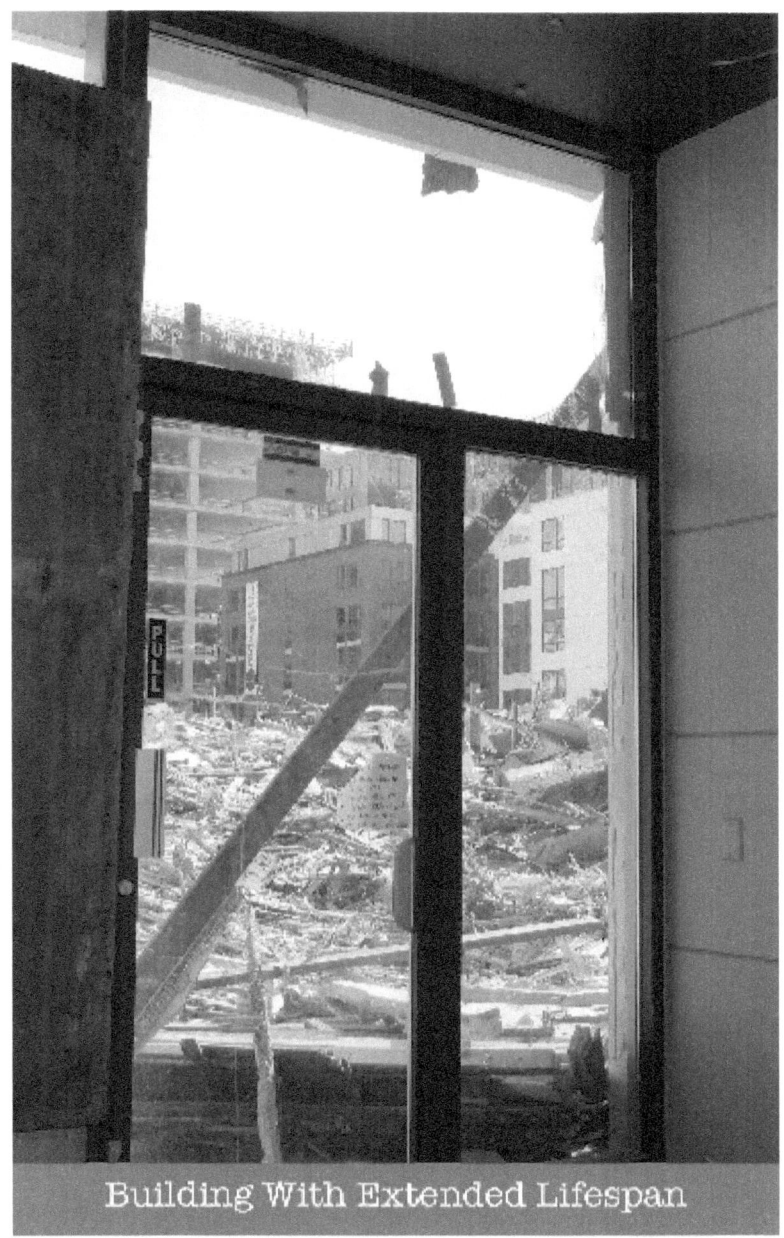

Building With Extended Lifespan

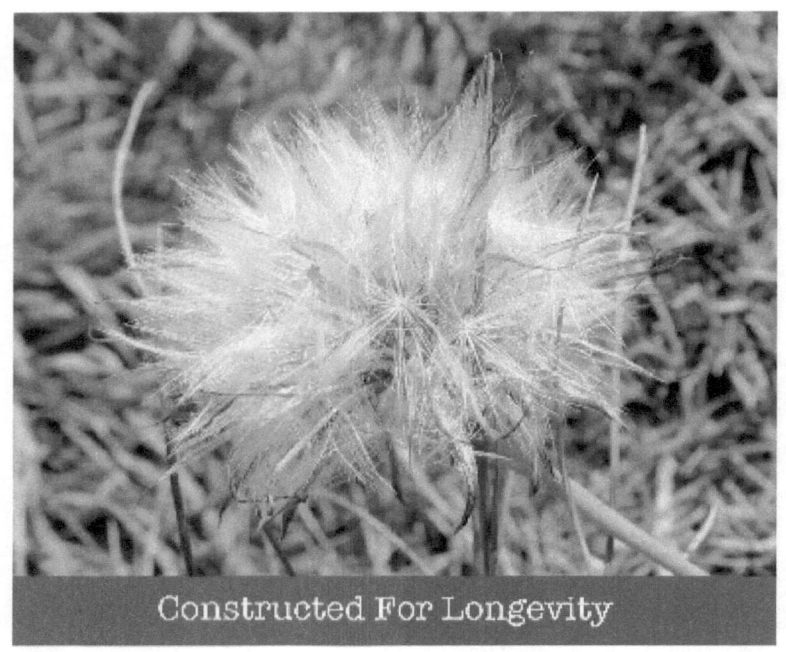
Constructed For Longevity

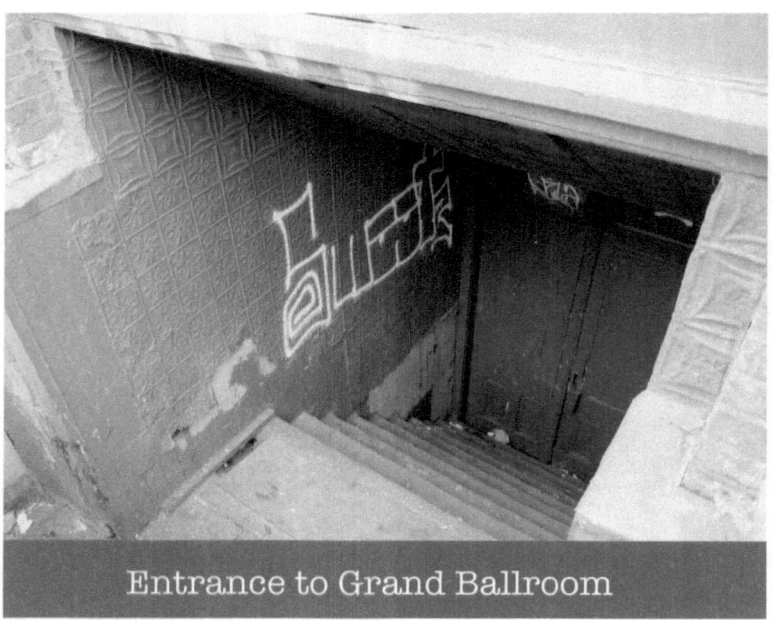
Entrance to Grand Ballroom

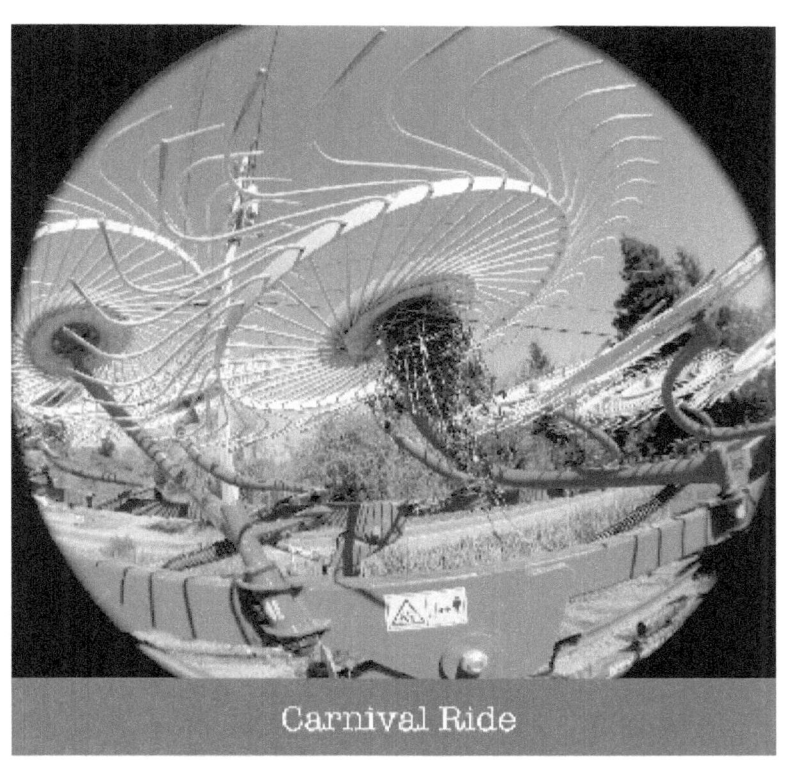

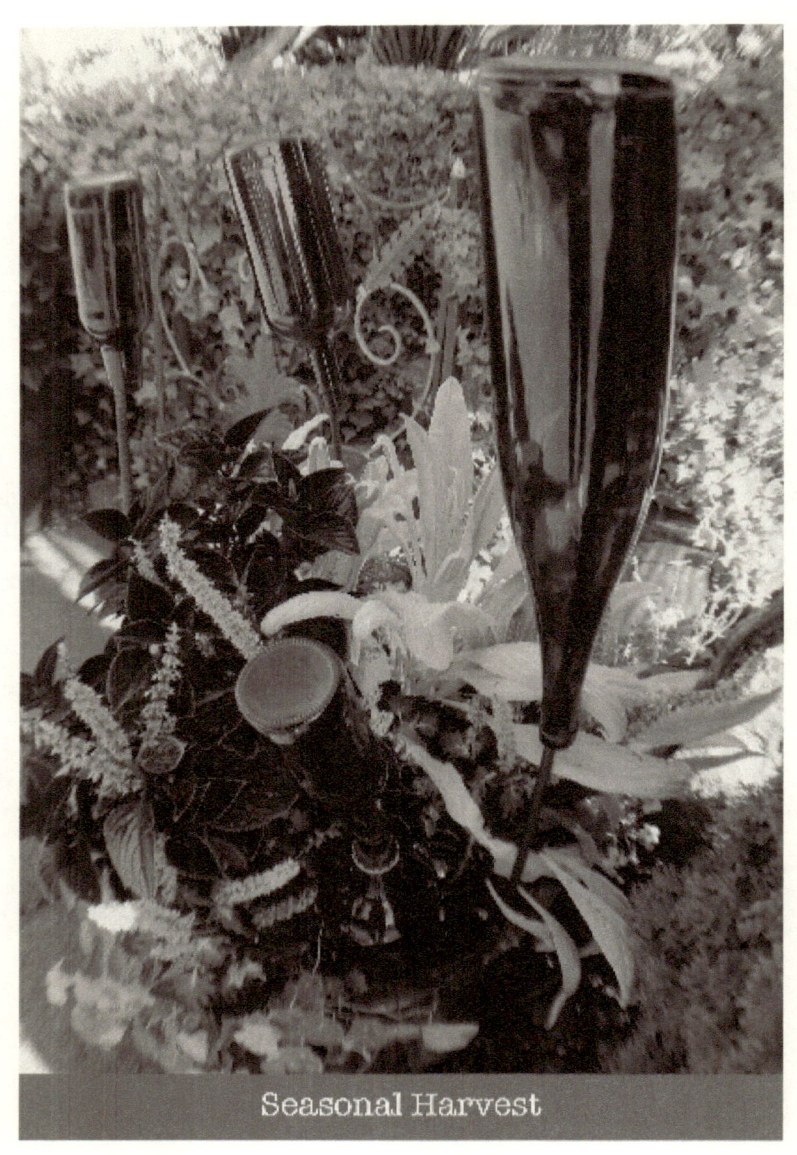
Seasonal Harvest

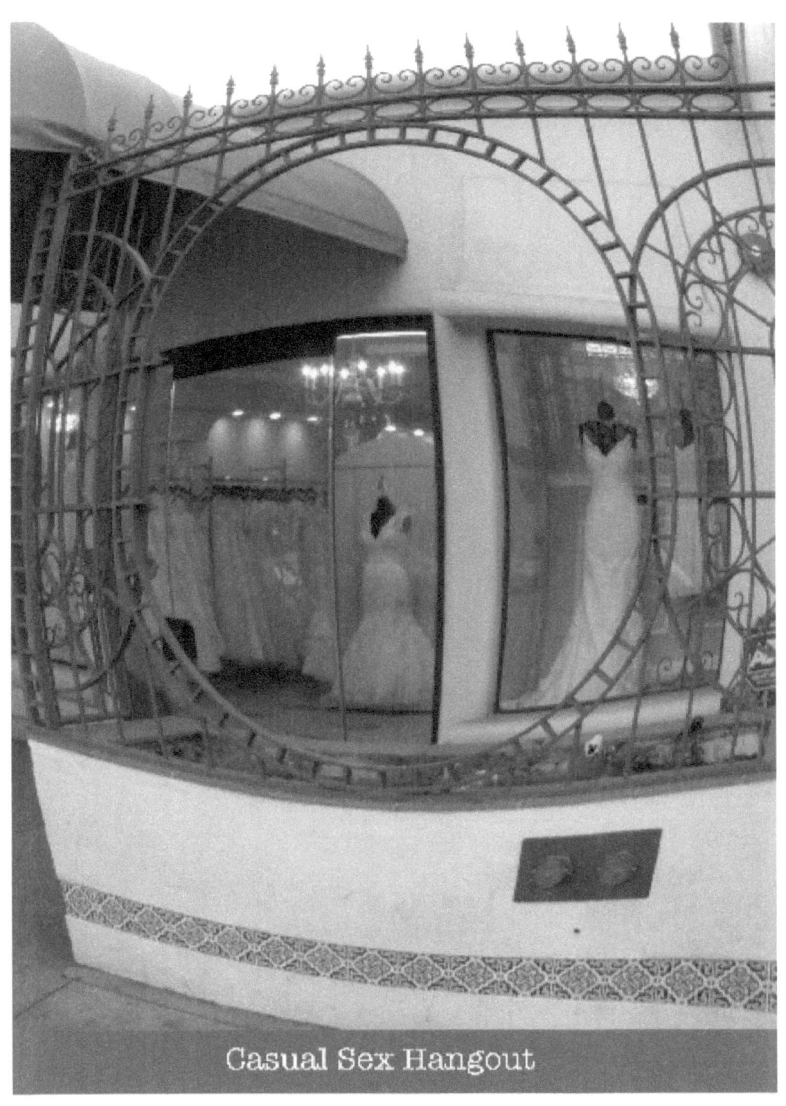

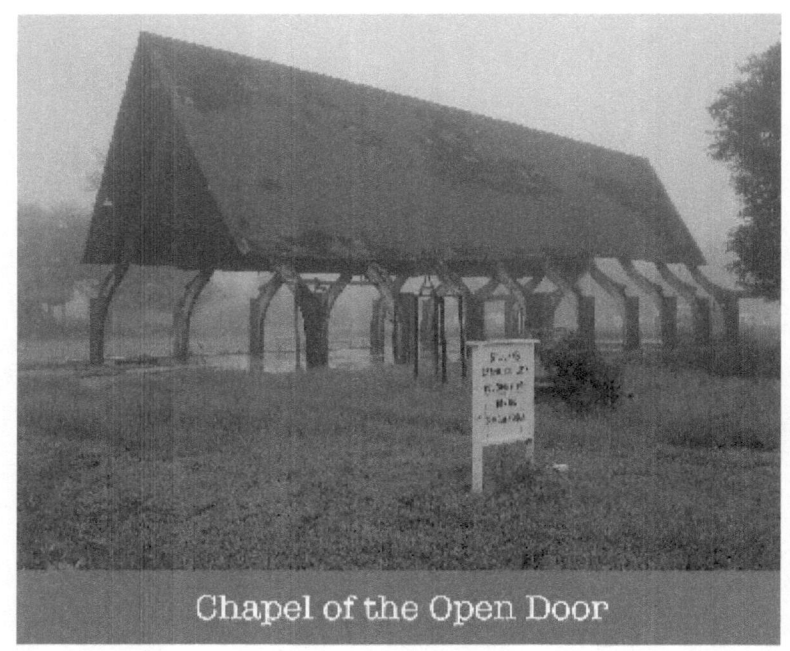
Chapel of the Open Door

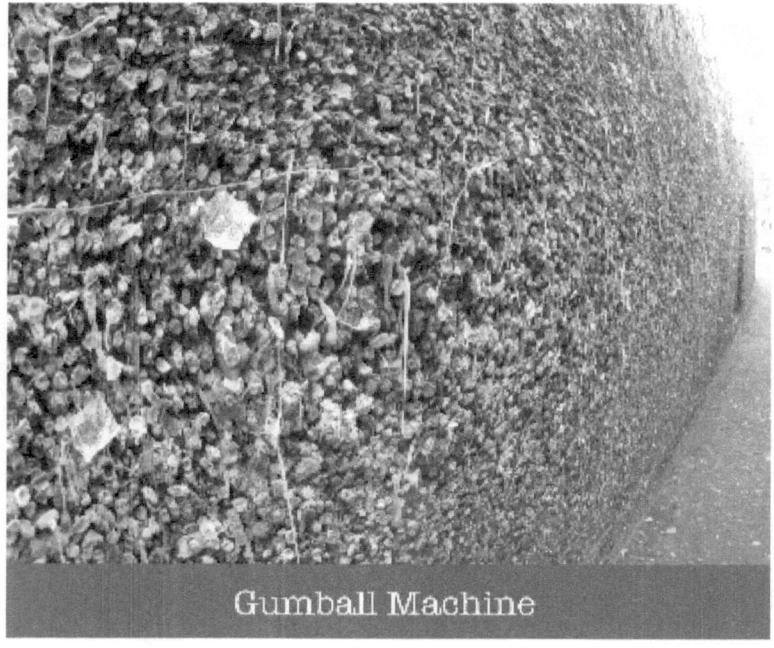
Gumball Machine

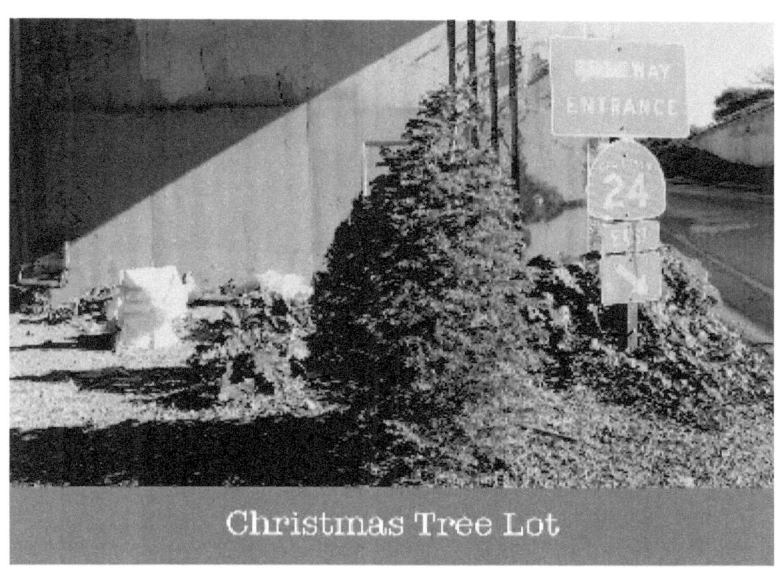
Christmas Tree Lot

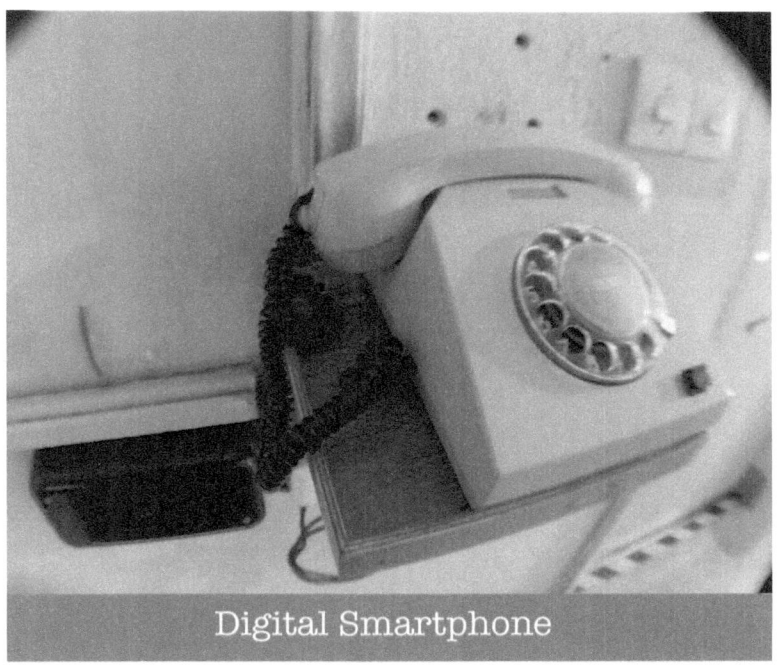
Digital Smartphone

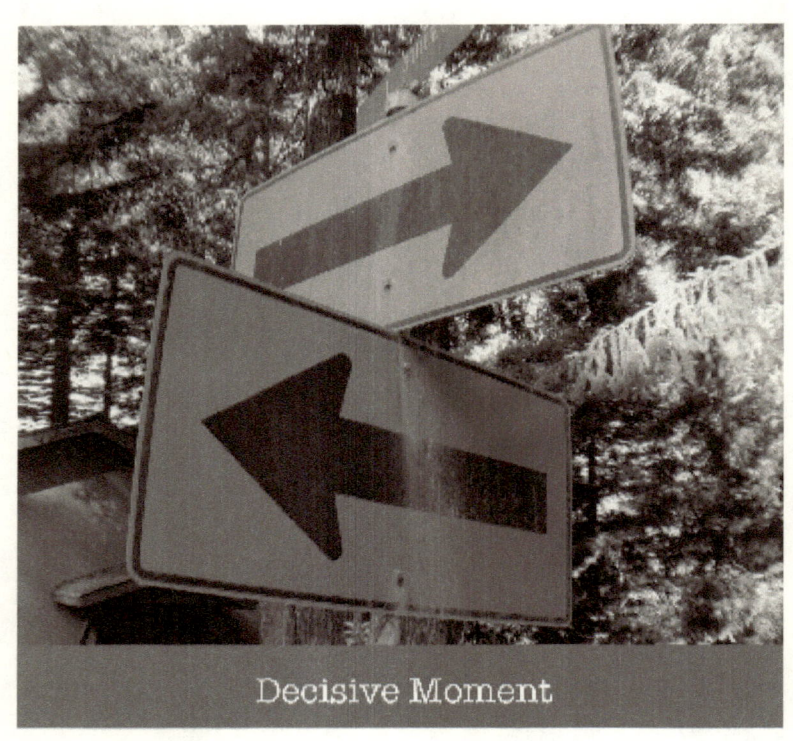

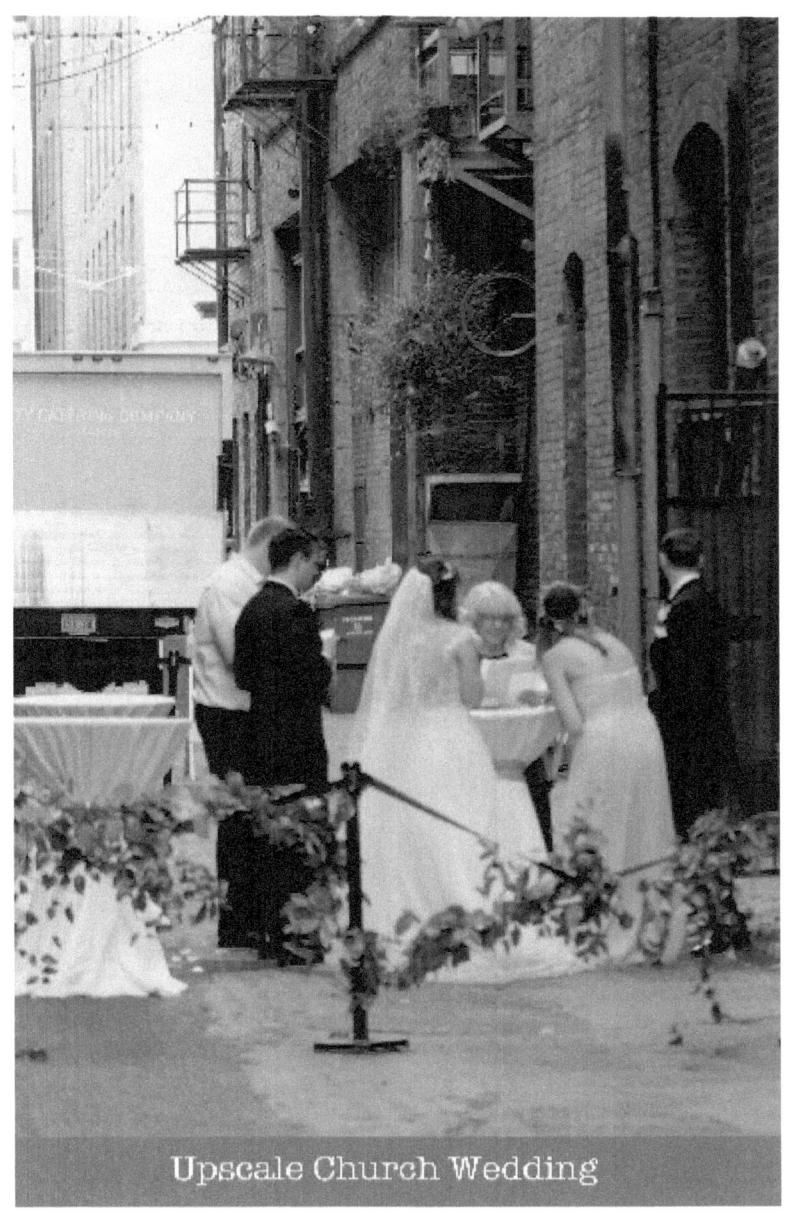
Upscale Church Wedding

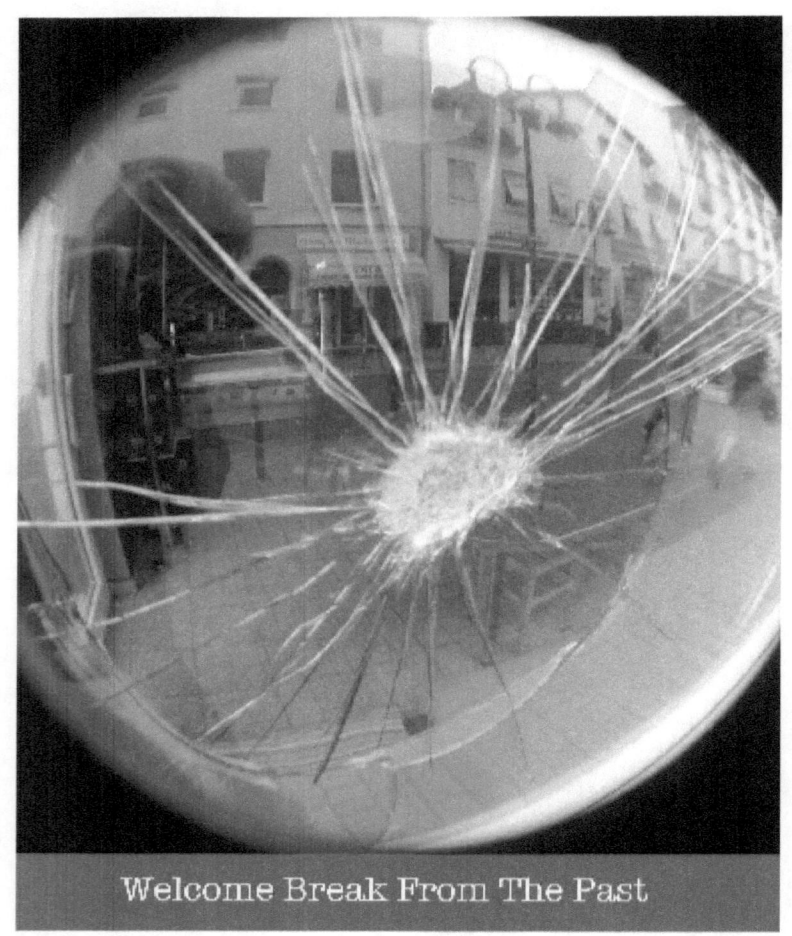

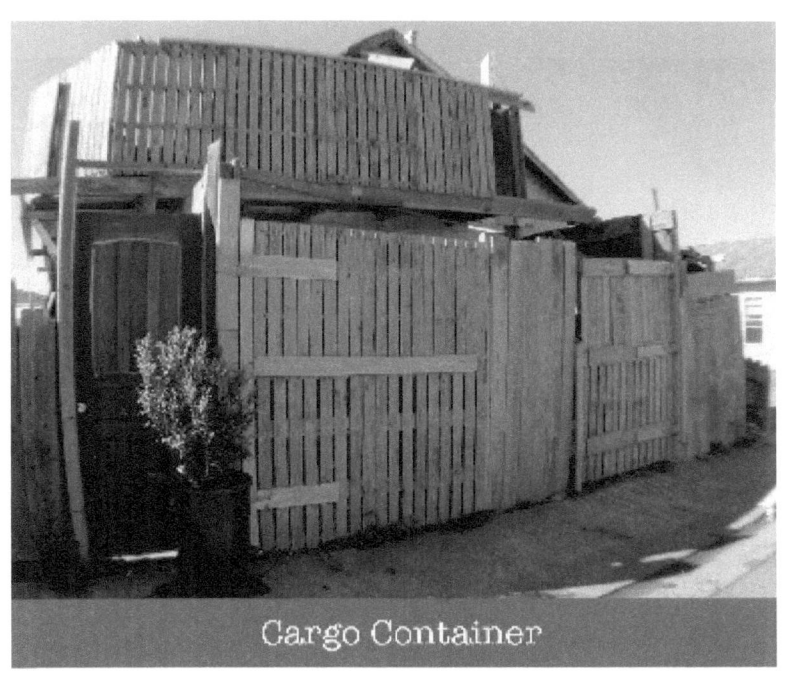
Cargo Container

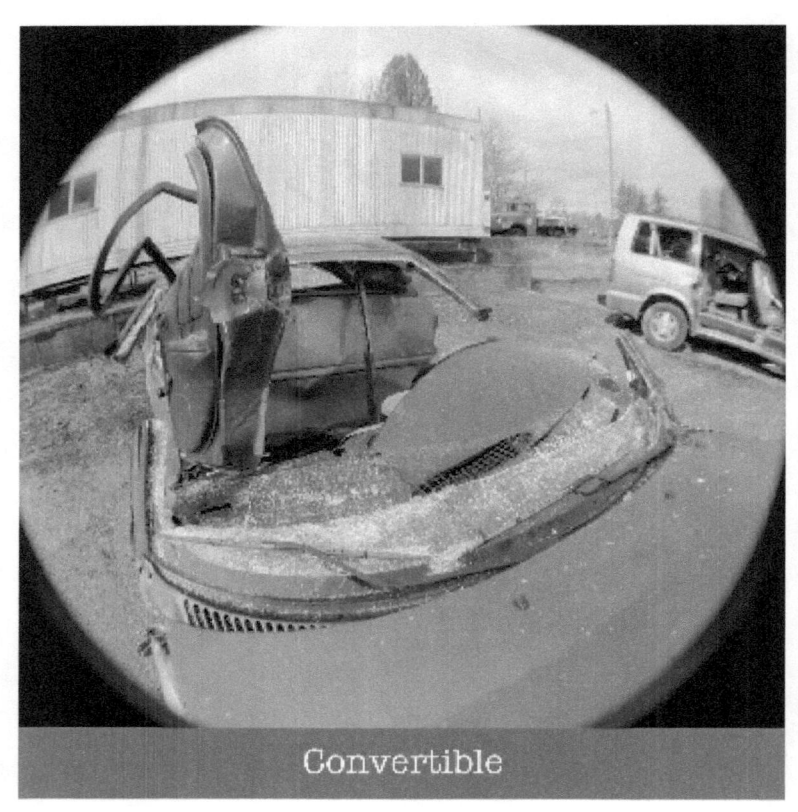

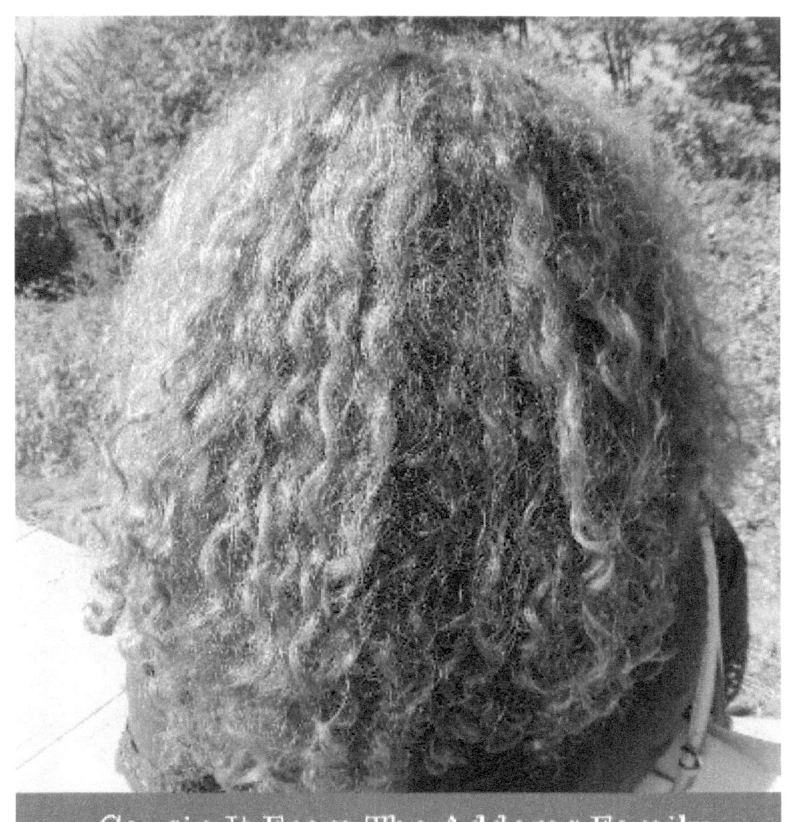
Cousin It From The Addams Family

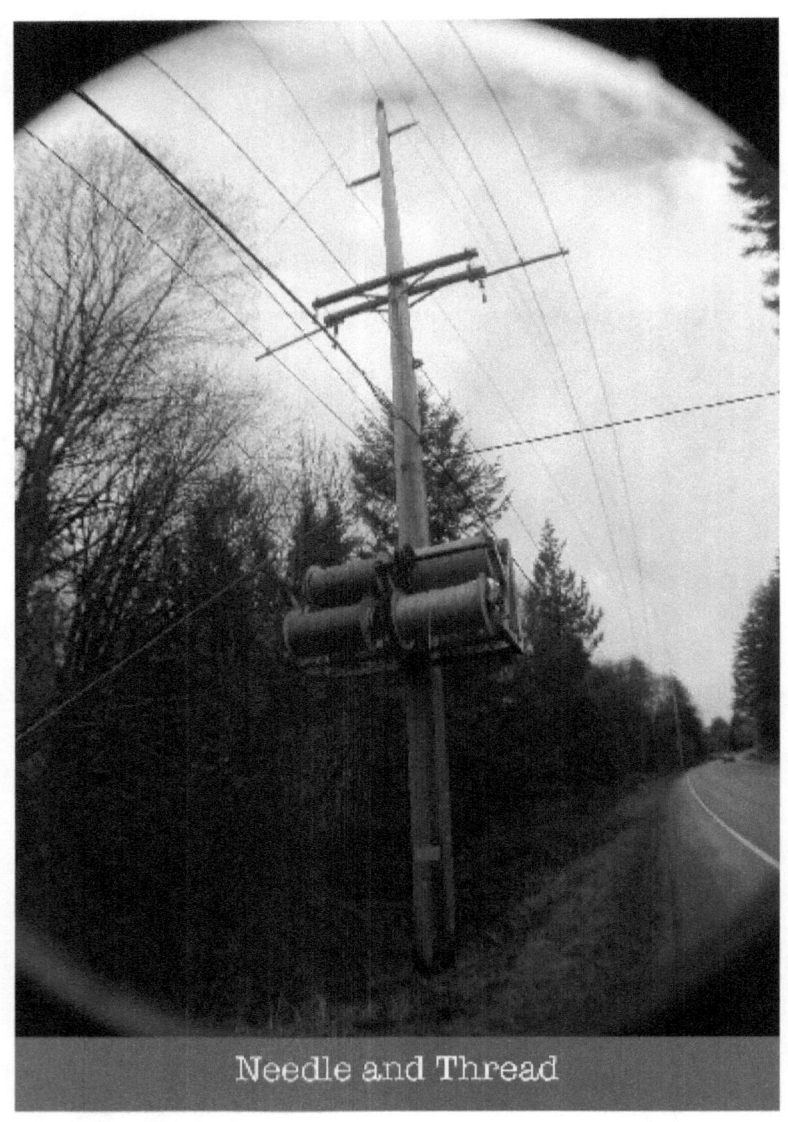

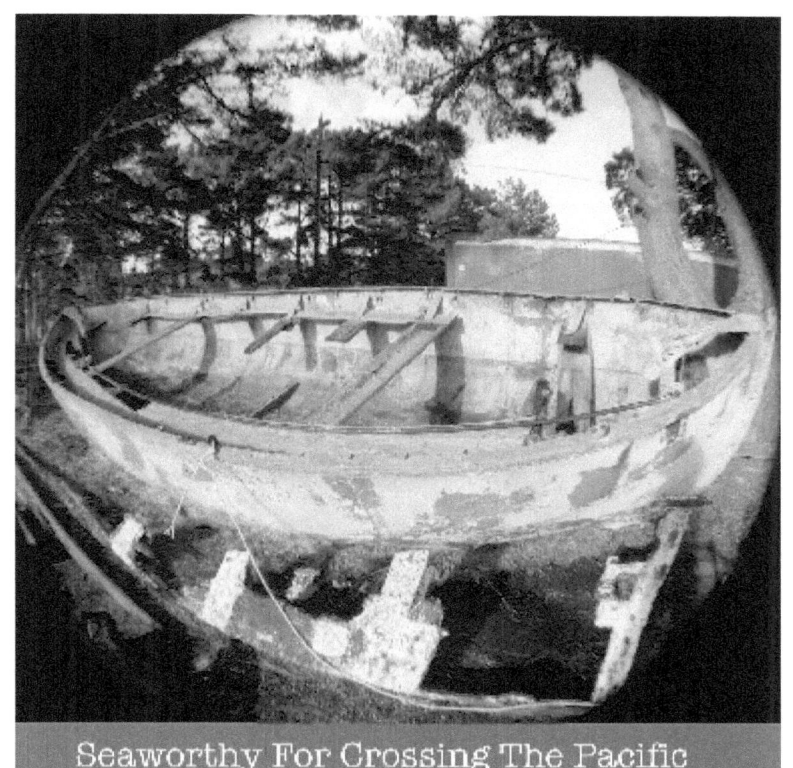
Seaworthy For Crossing The Pacific

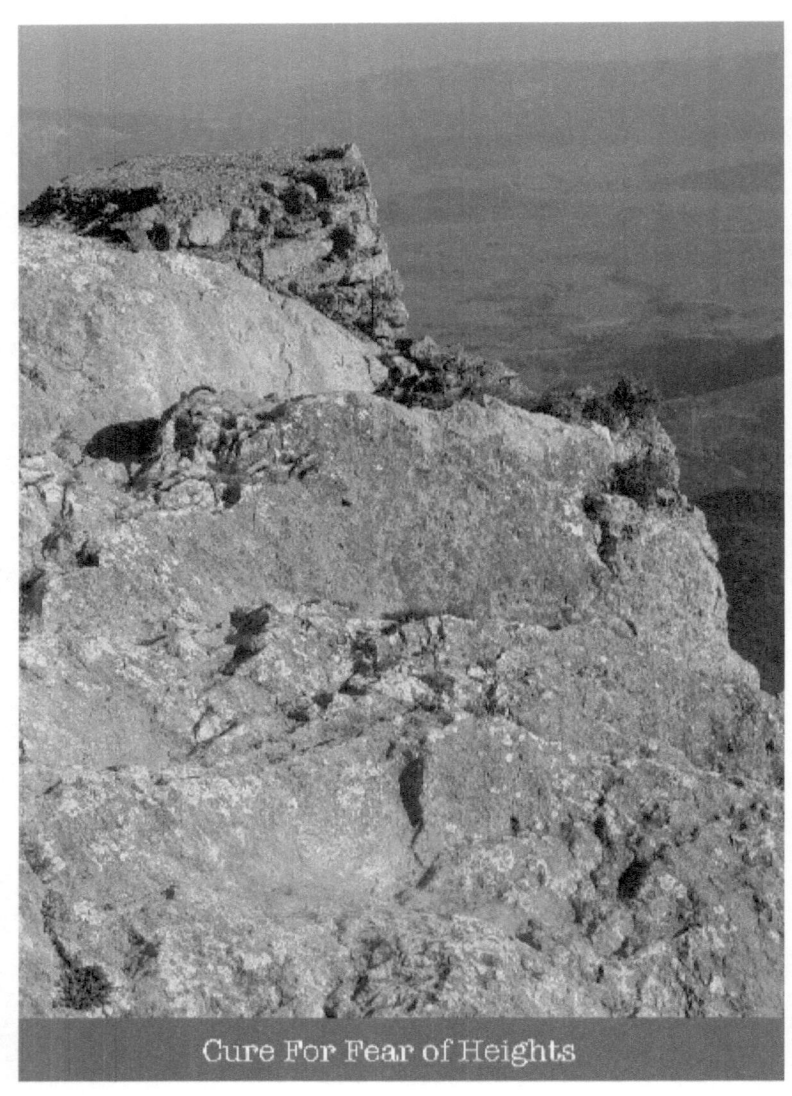
Cure For Fear of Heights

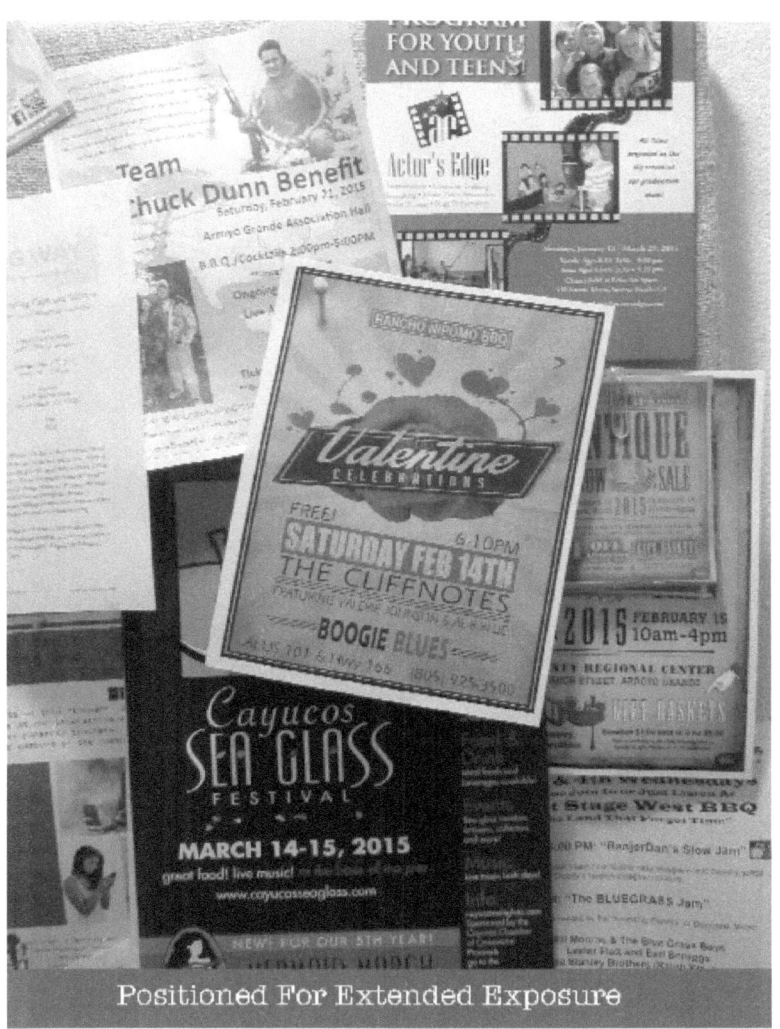

Positioned For Extended Exposure

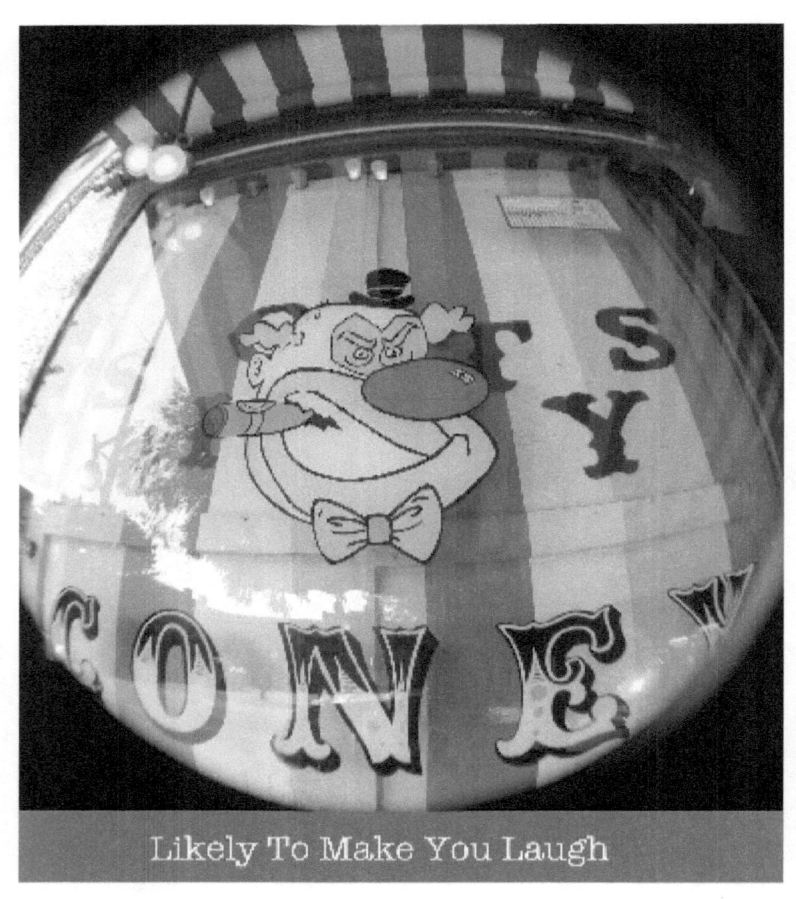
Likely To Make You Laugh

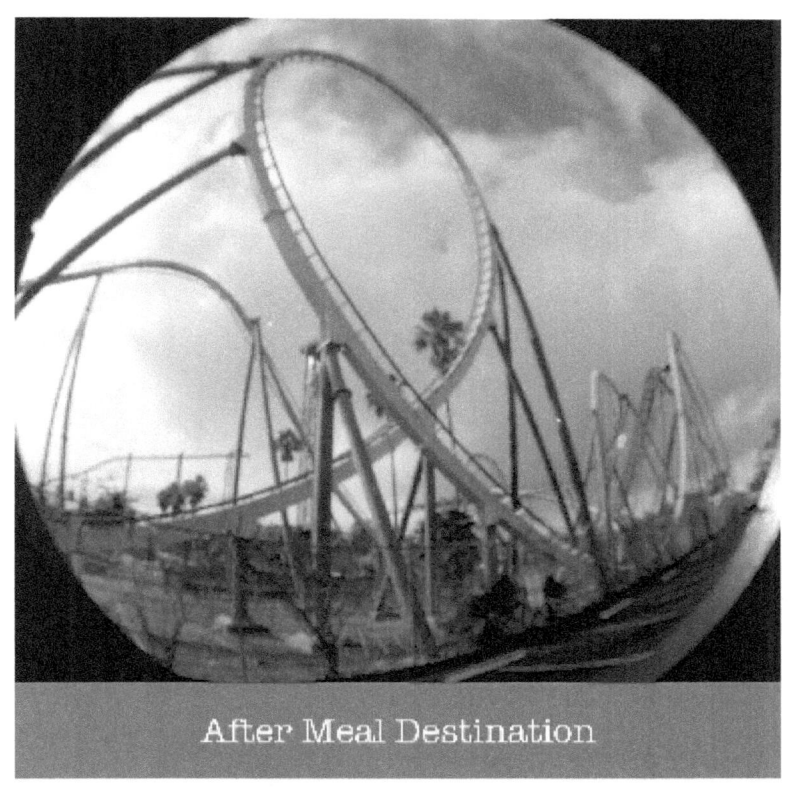

After Meal Destination

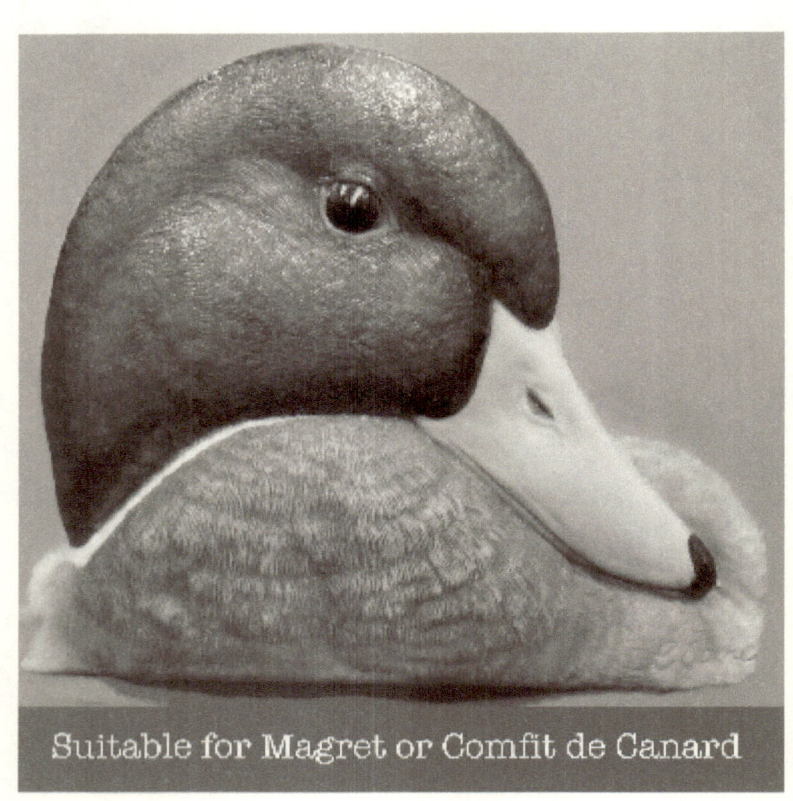

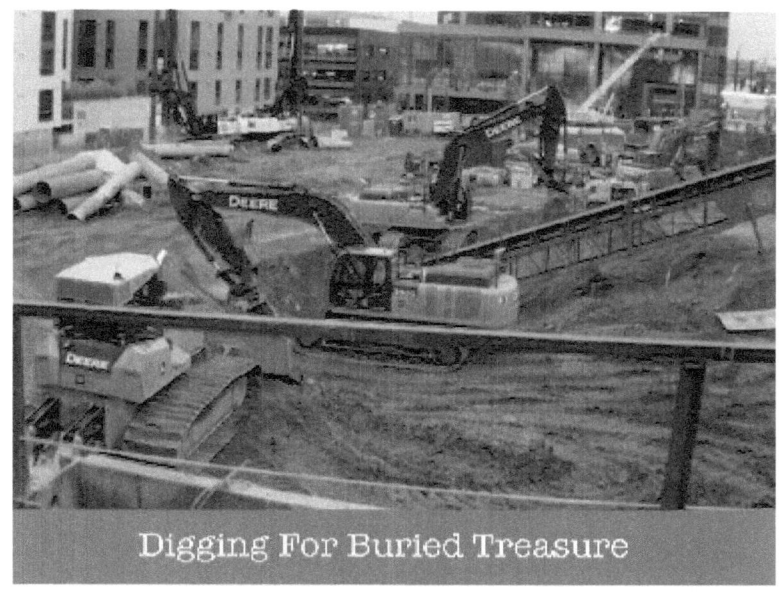
Digging For Buried Treasure

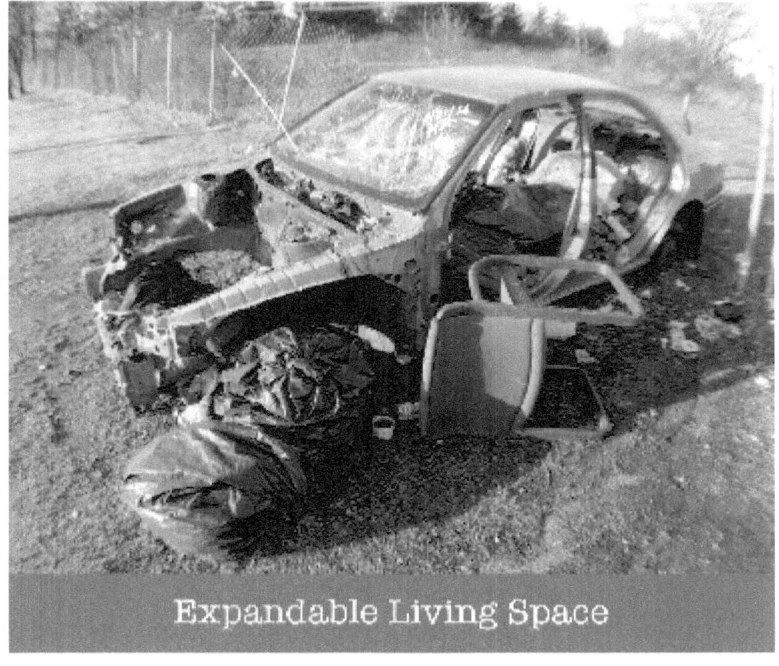
Expandable Living Space

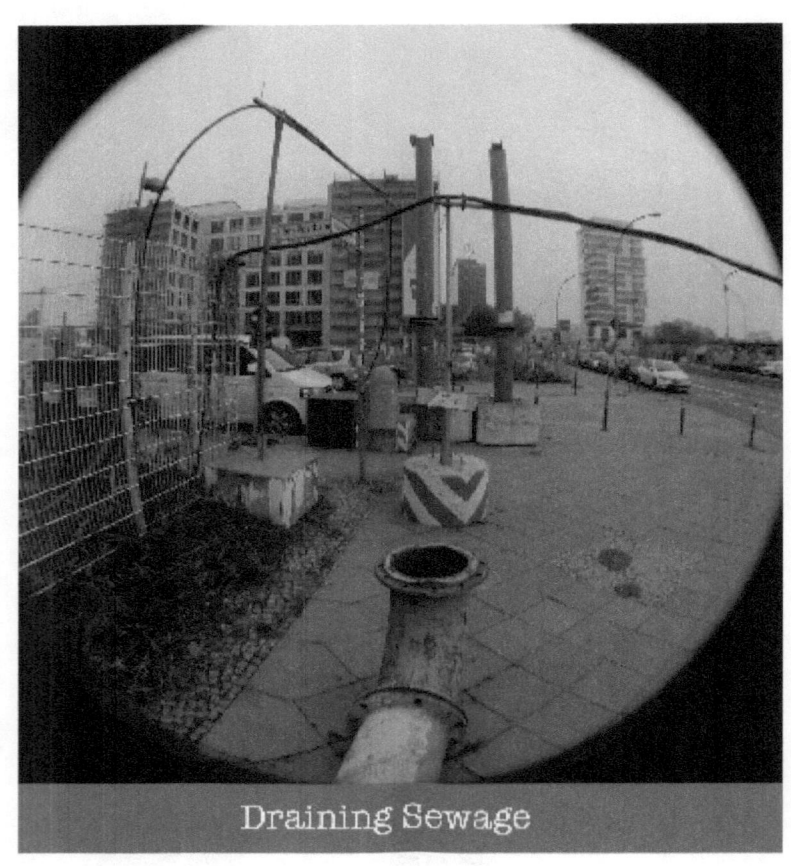
Draining Sewage

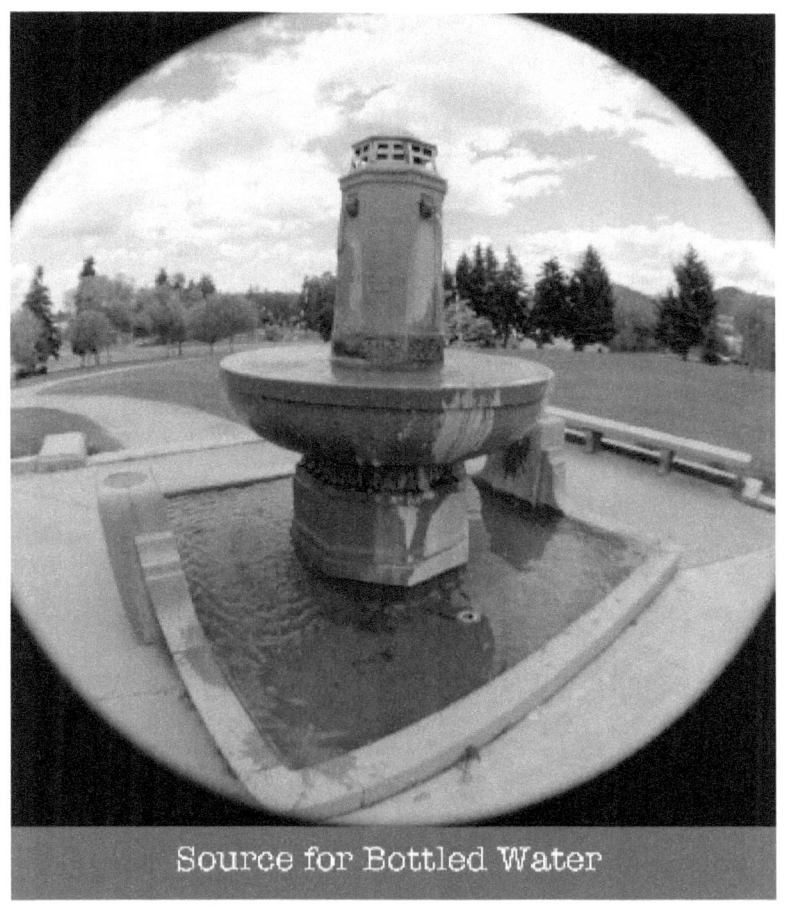
Source for Bottled Water

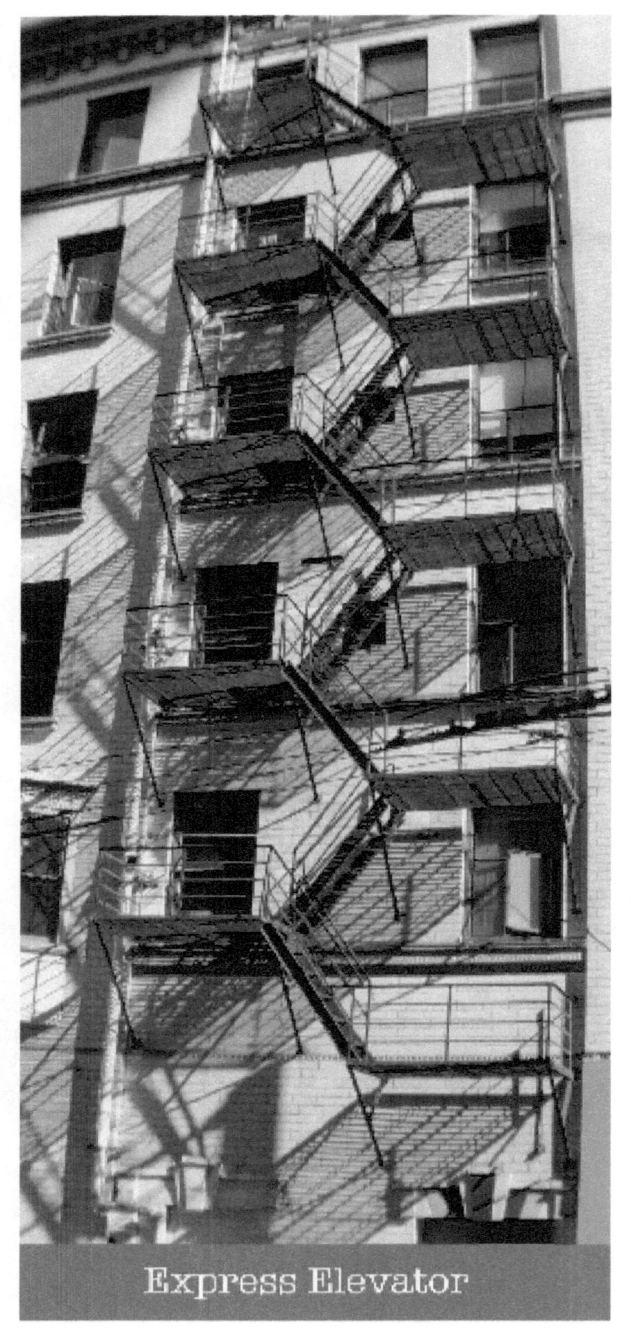
Express Elevator

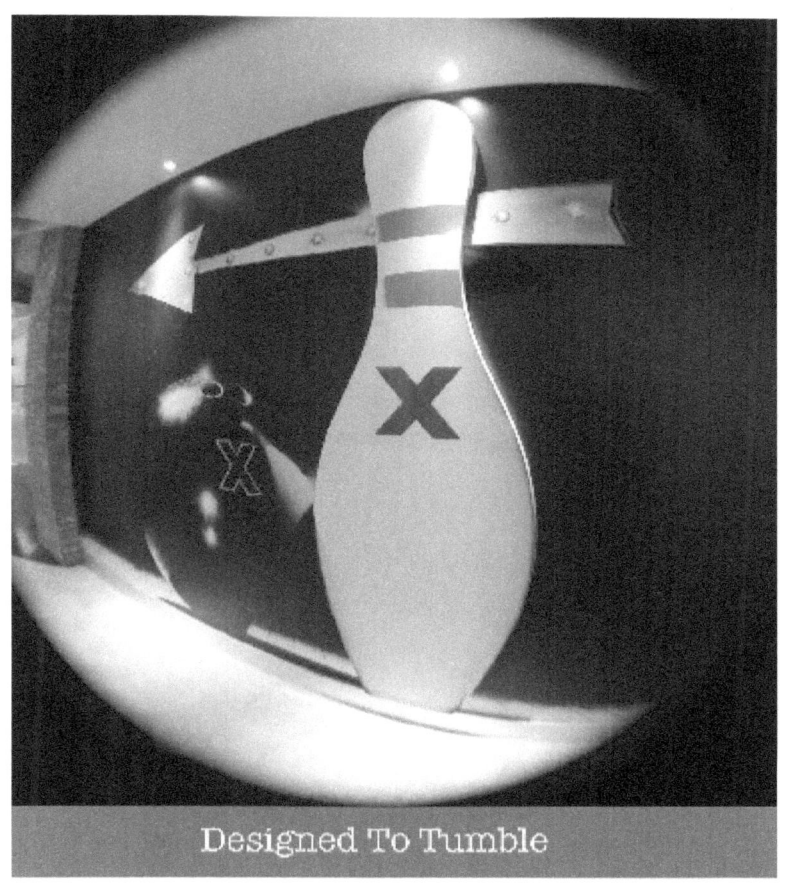

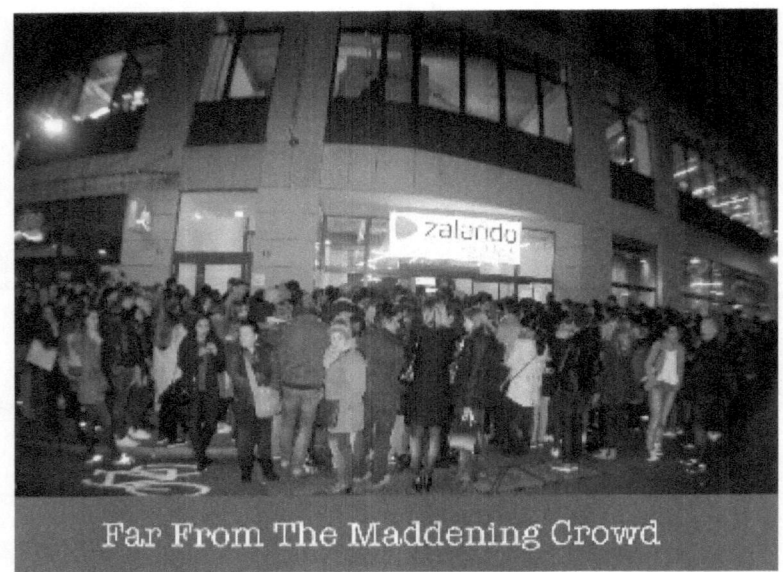
Far From The Maddening Crowd

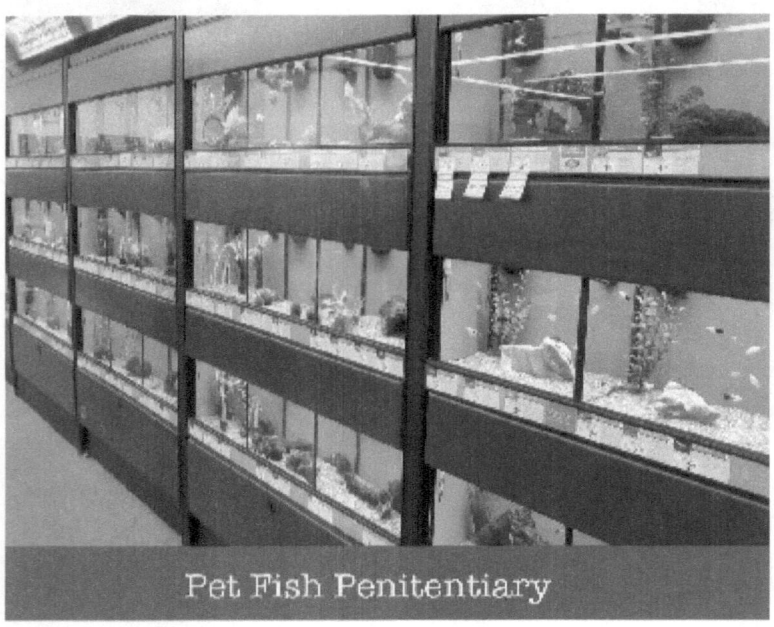
Pet Fish Penitentiary

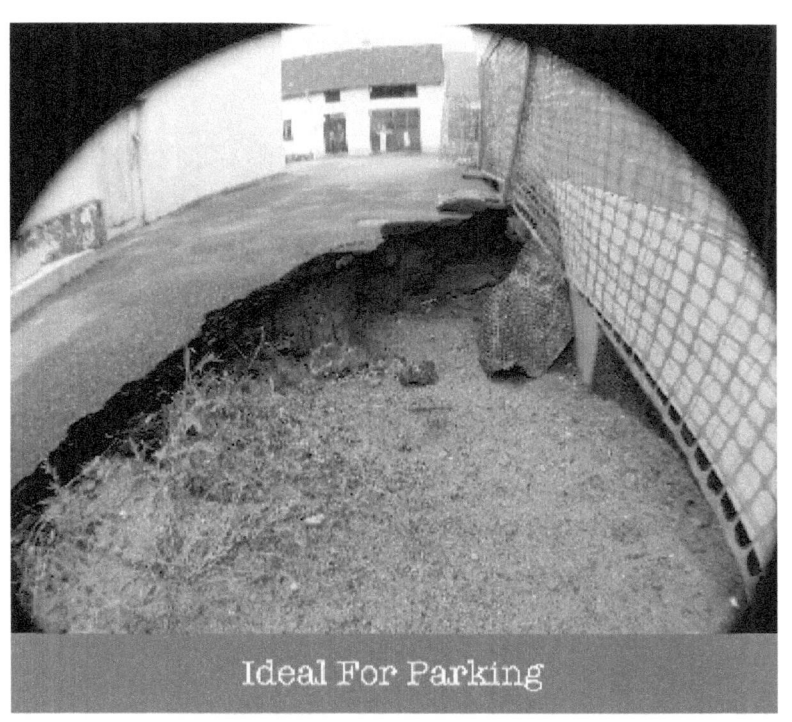
Ideal For Parking

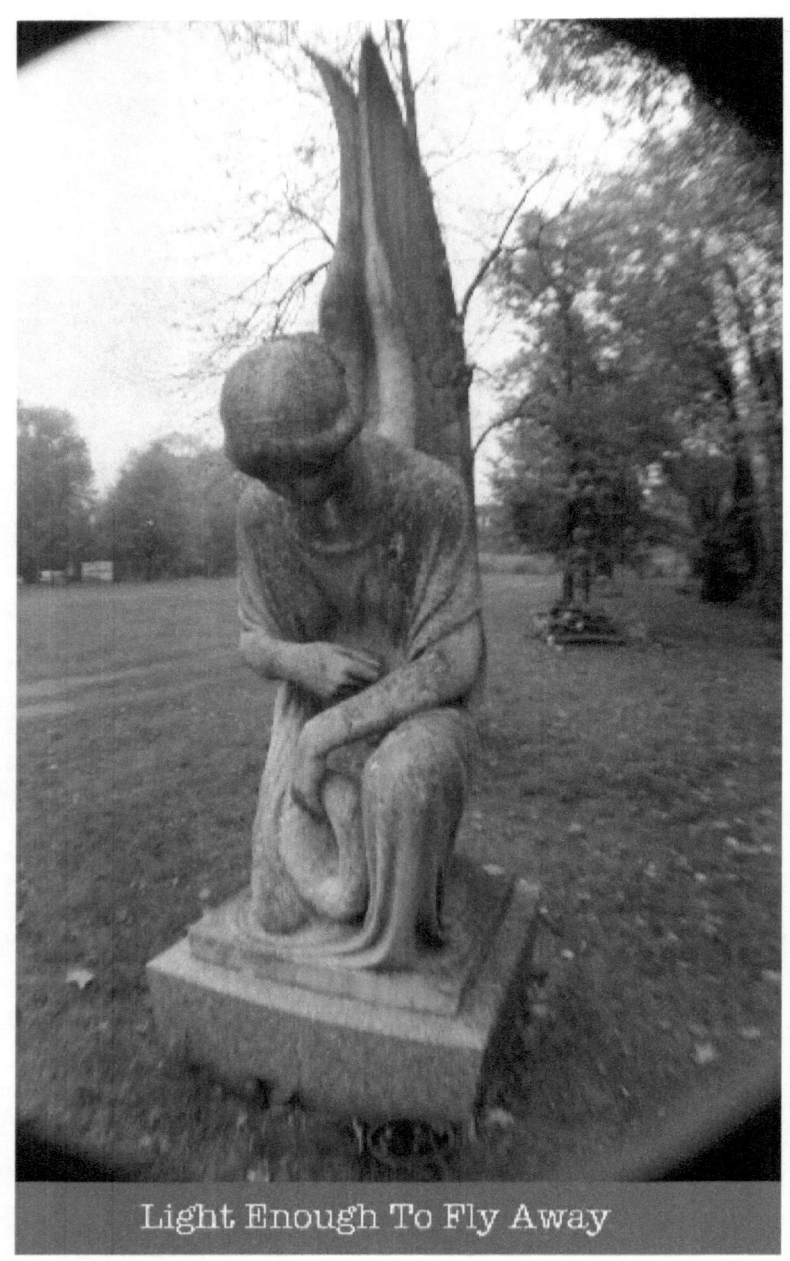

Light Enough To Fly Away

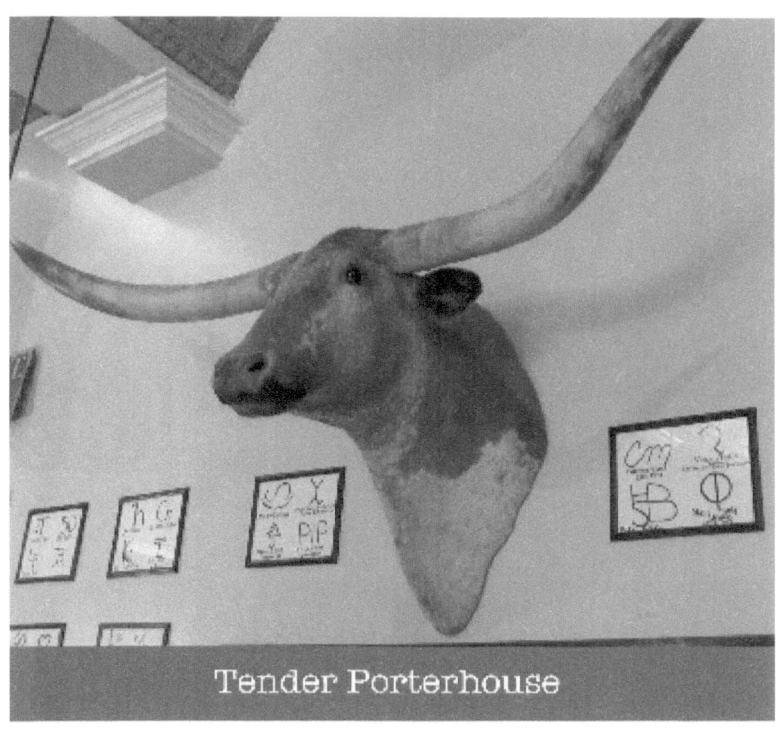
Tender Porterhouse

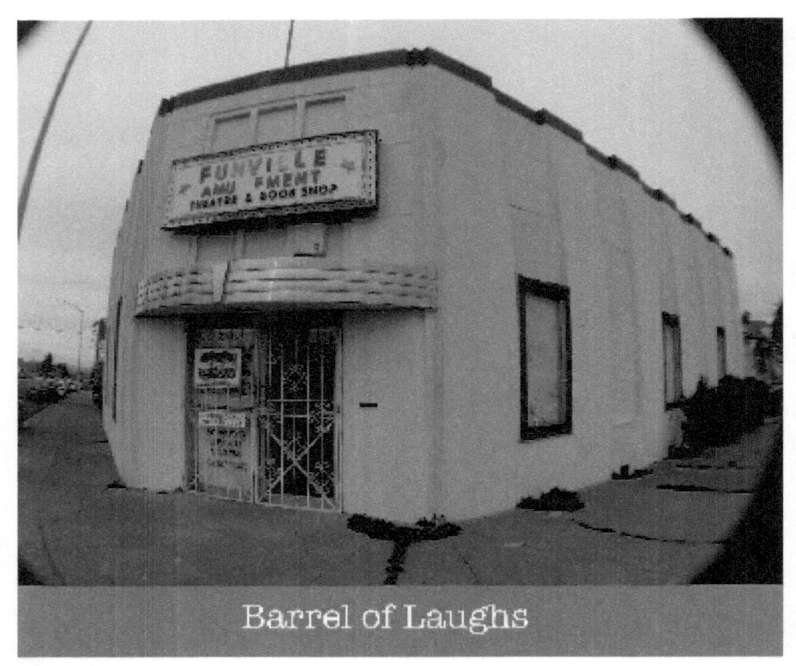
Barrel of Laughs

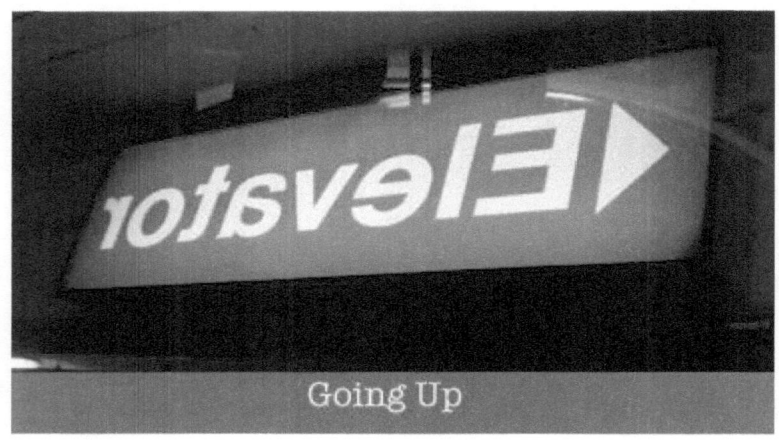
Going Up

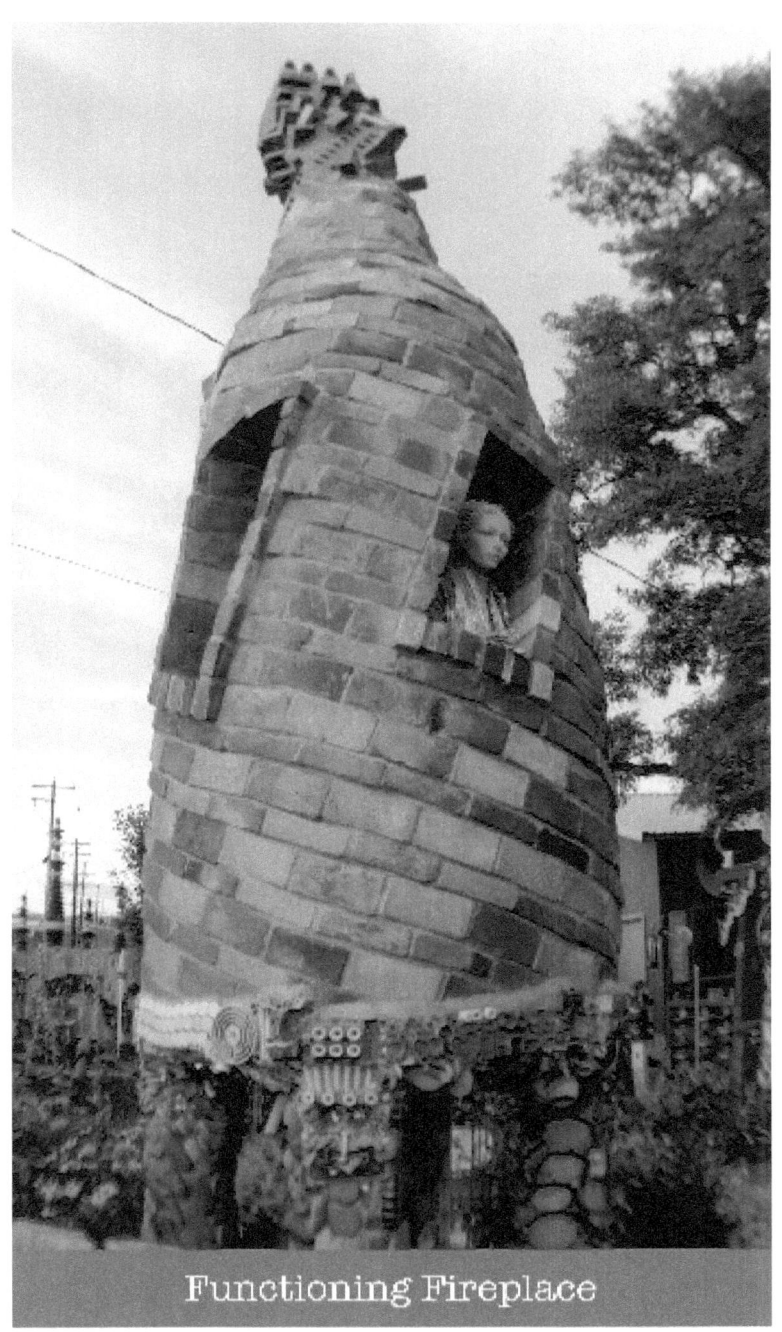

Functioning Fireplace

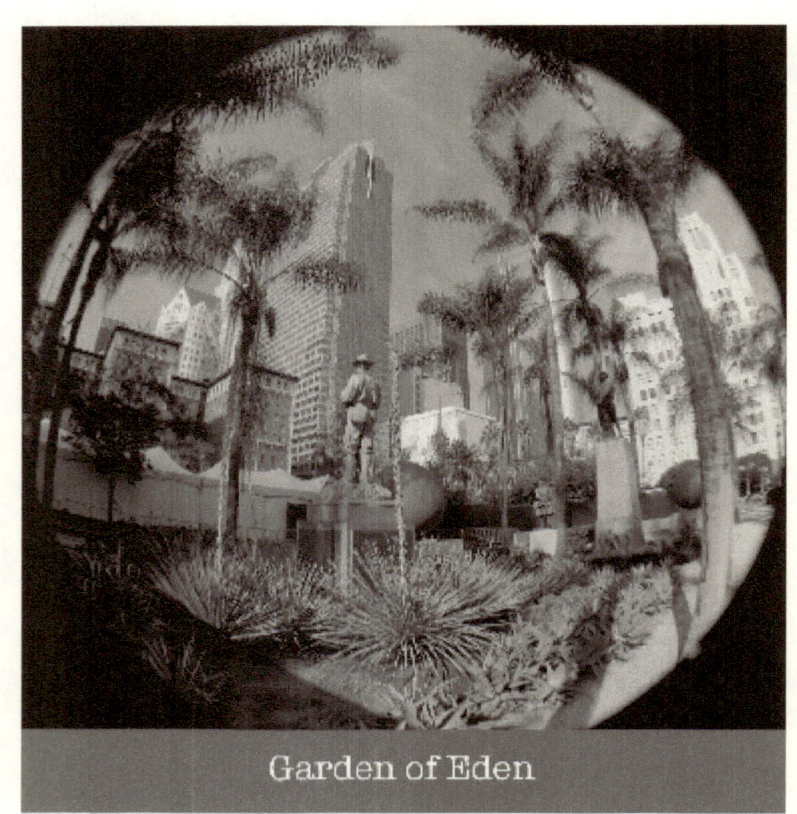

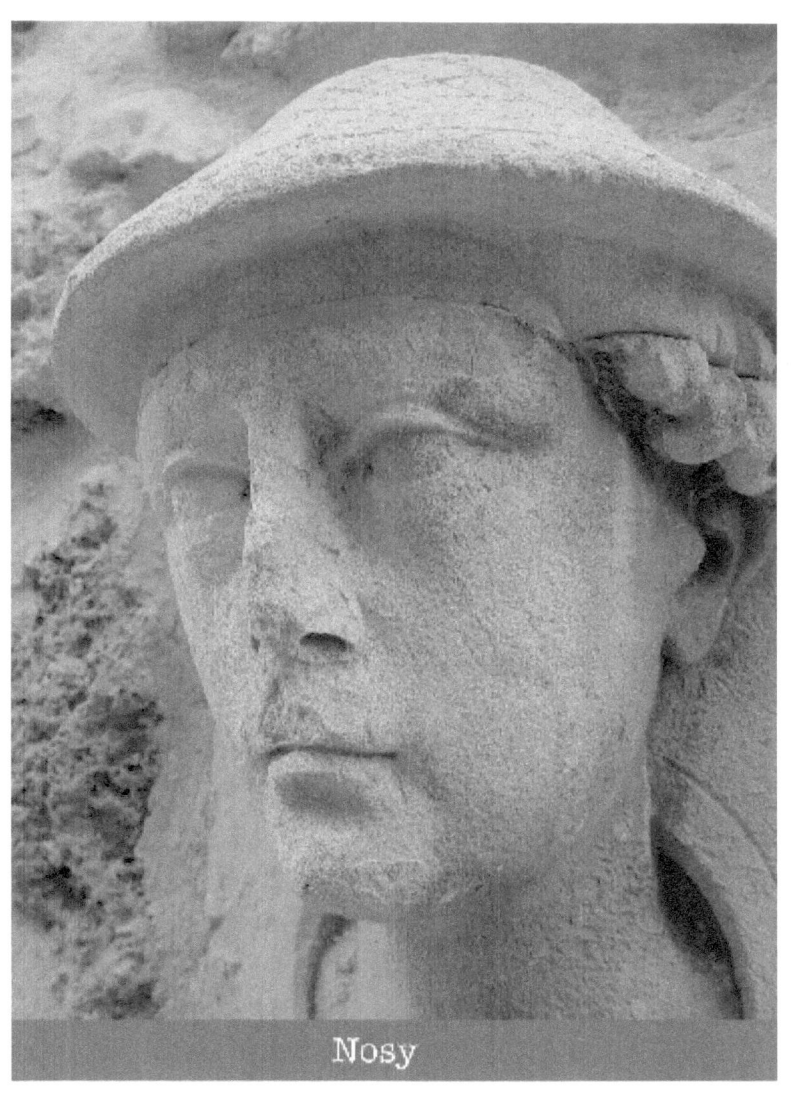
Nosy

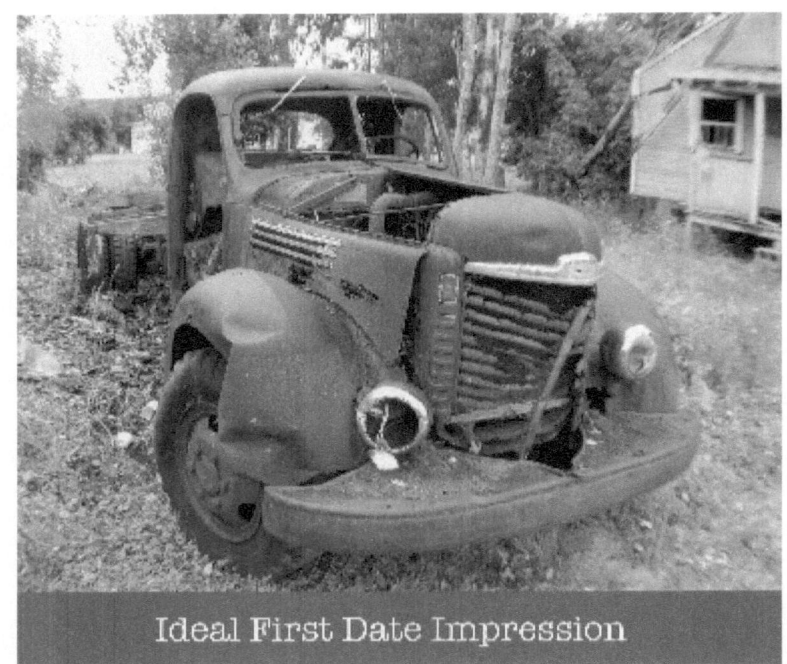
Ideal First Date Impression

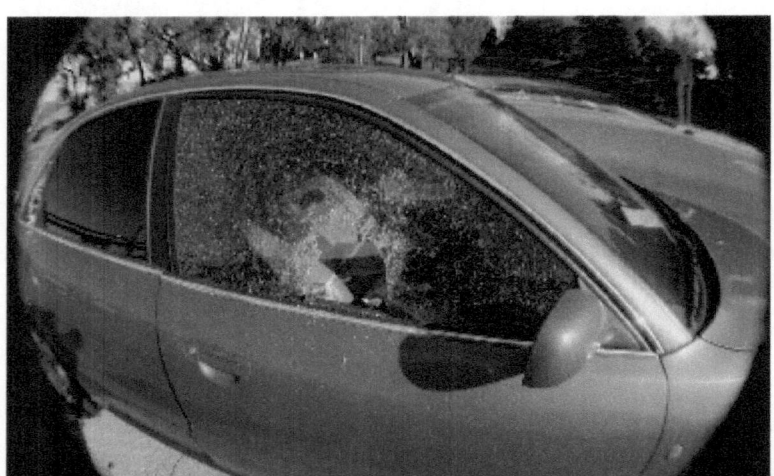
Aesthetic Solution For Locating Lost Keys

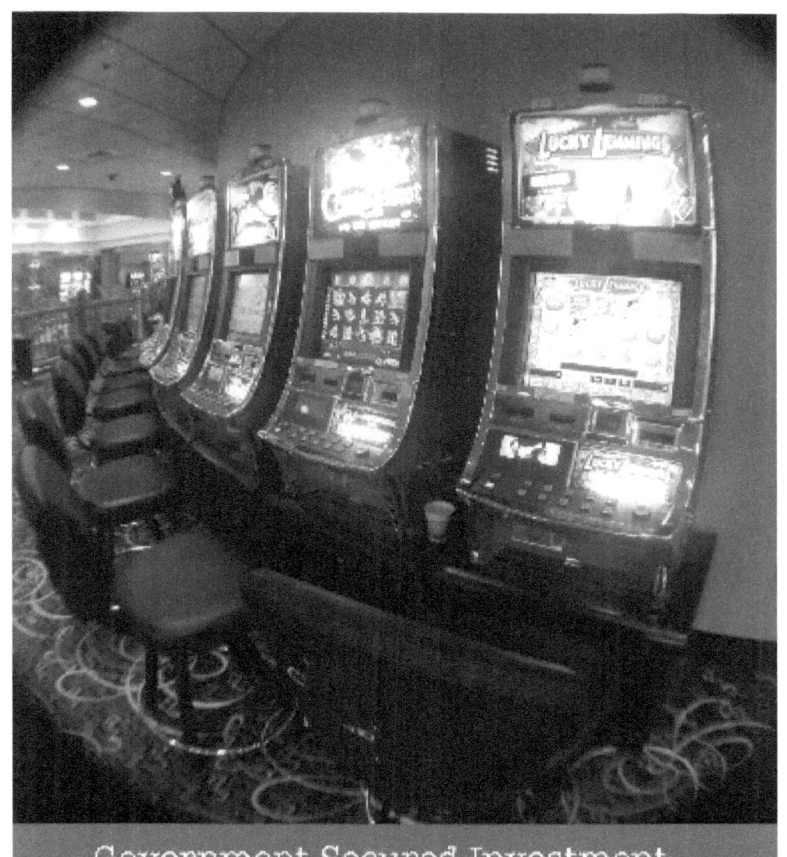
Government Secured Investment

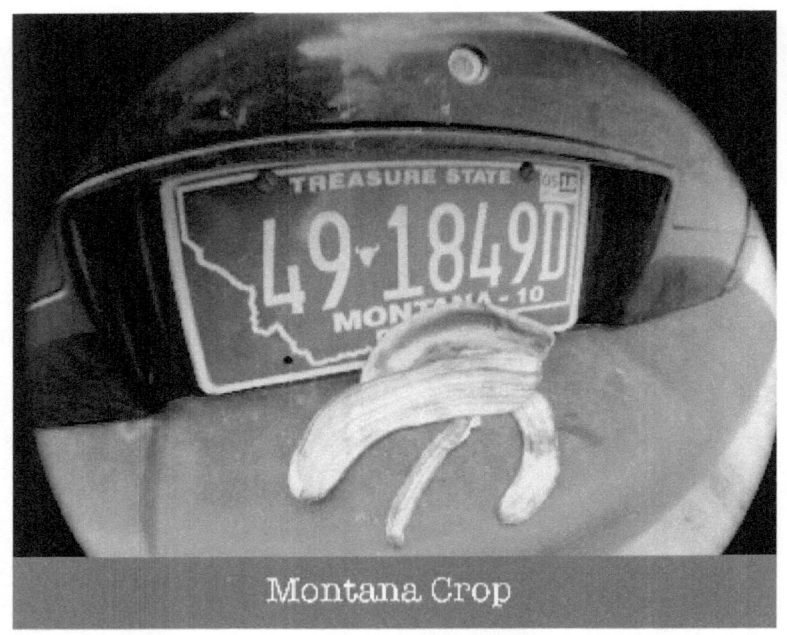

Montana Crop

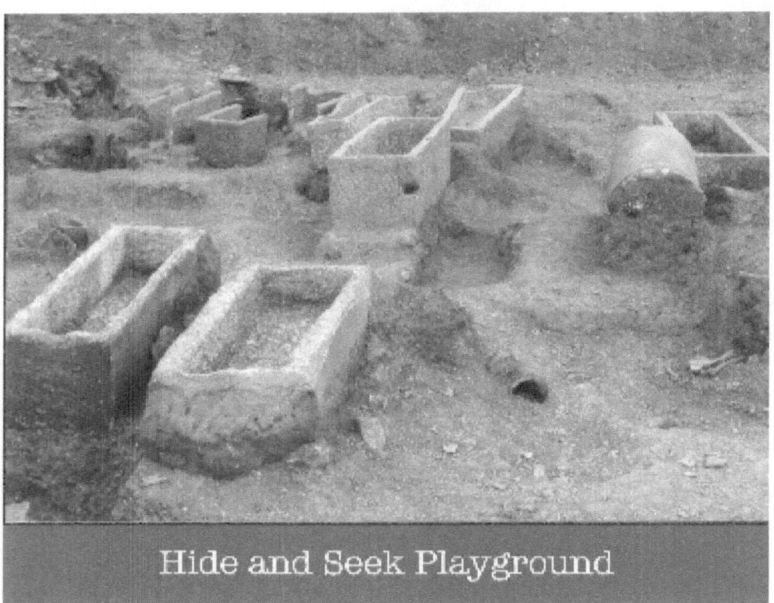

Hide and Seek Playground

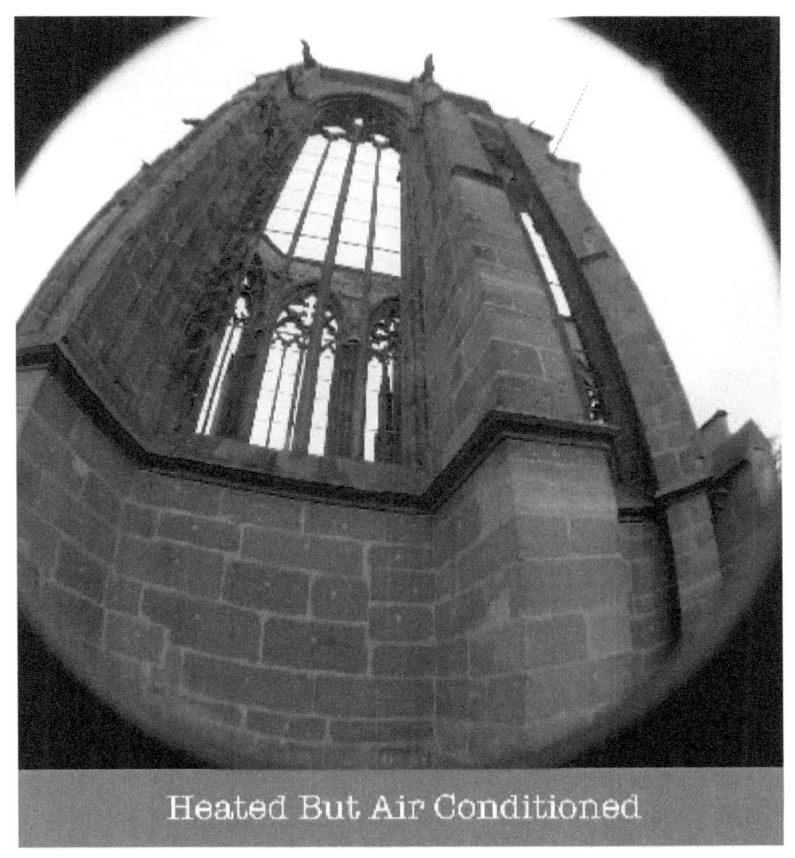

Heated But Air Conditioned

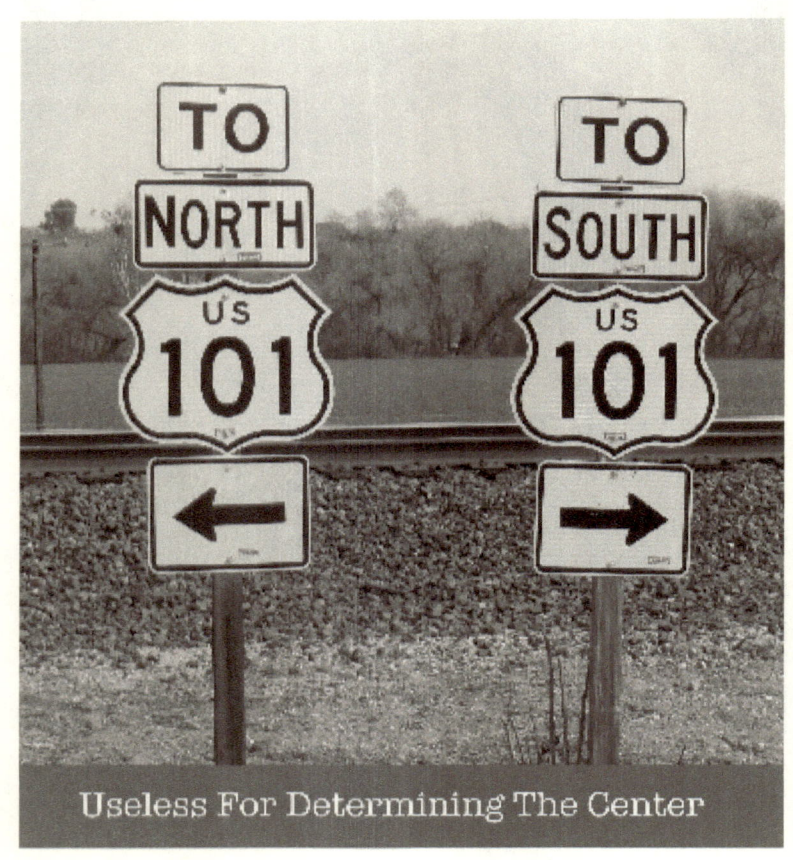

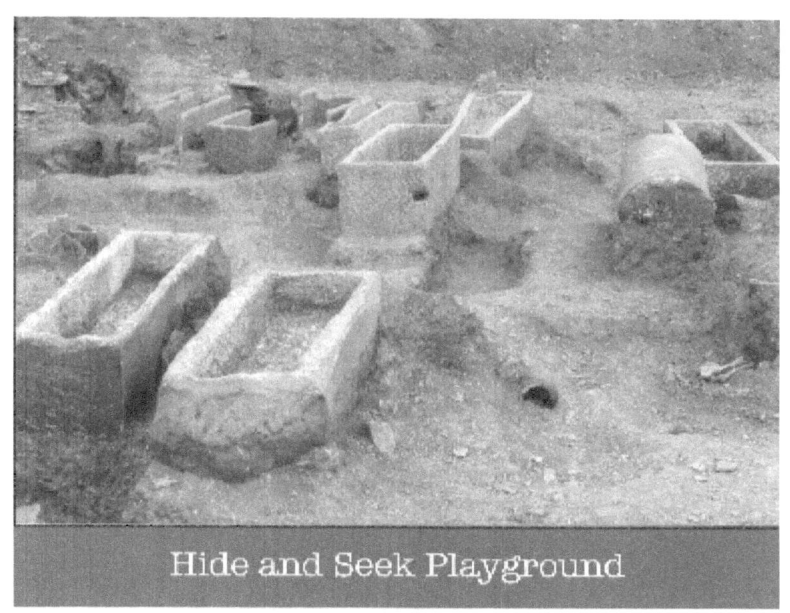
Hide and Seek Playground

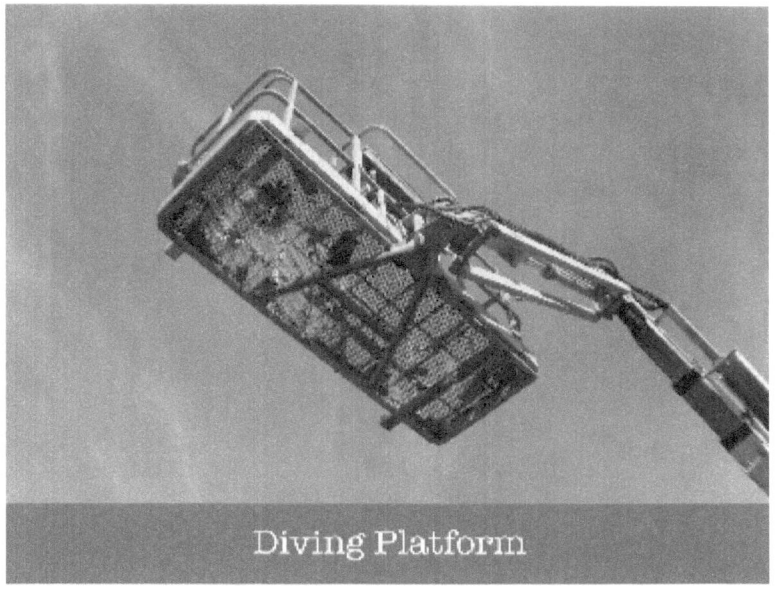
Diving Platform

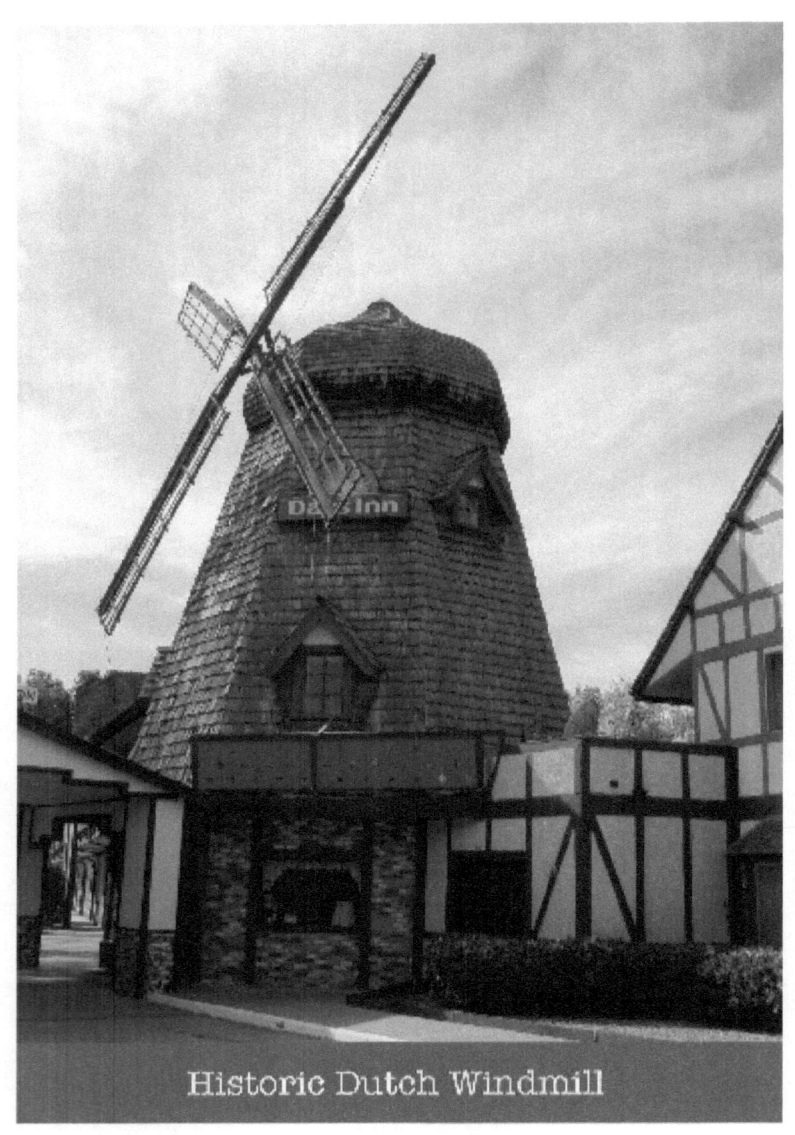
Historic Dutch Windmill

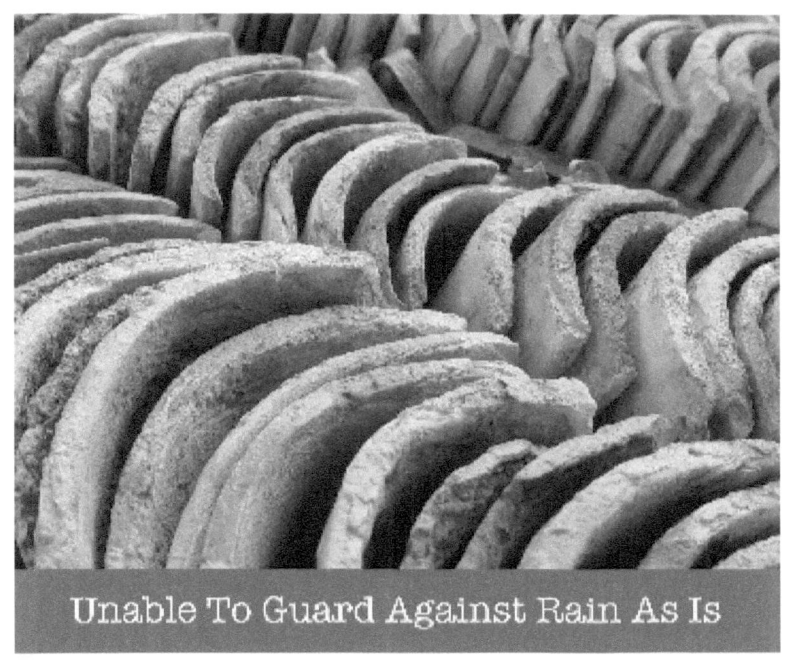

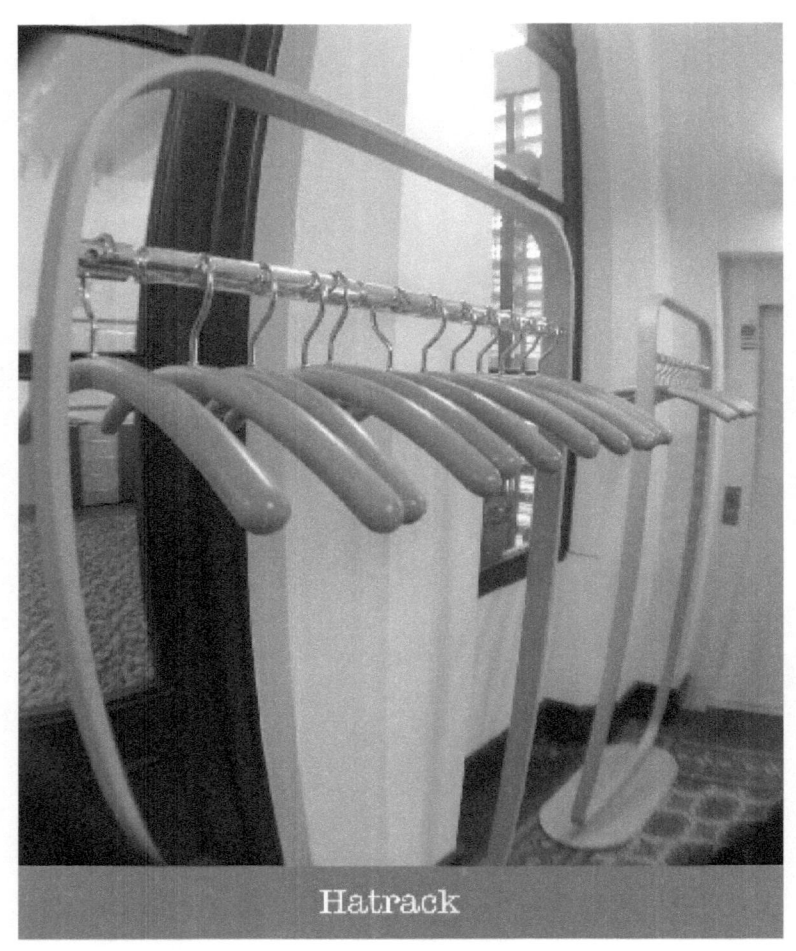

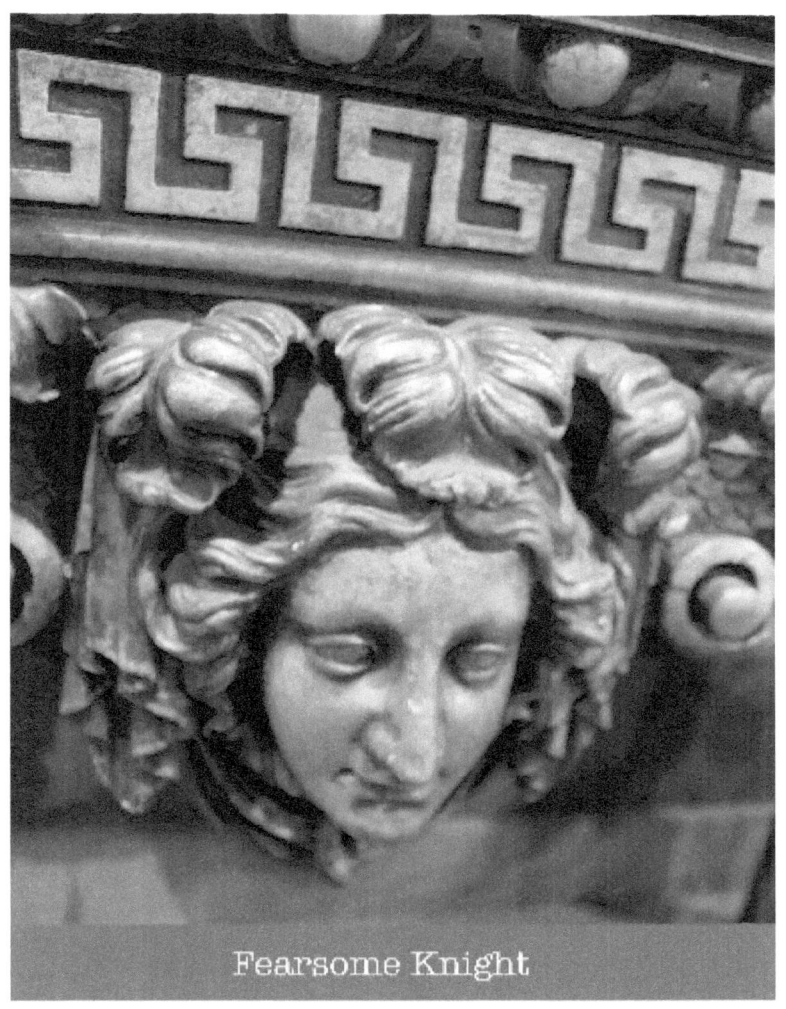
Fearsome Knight

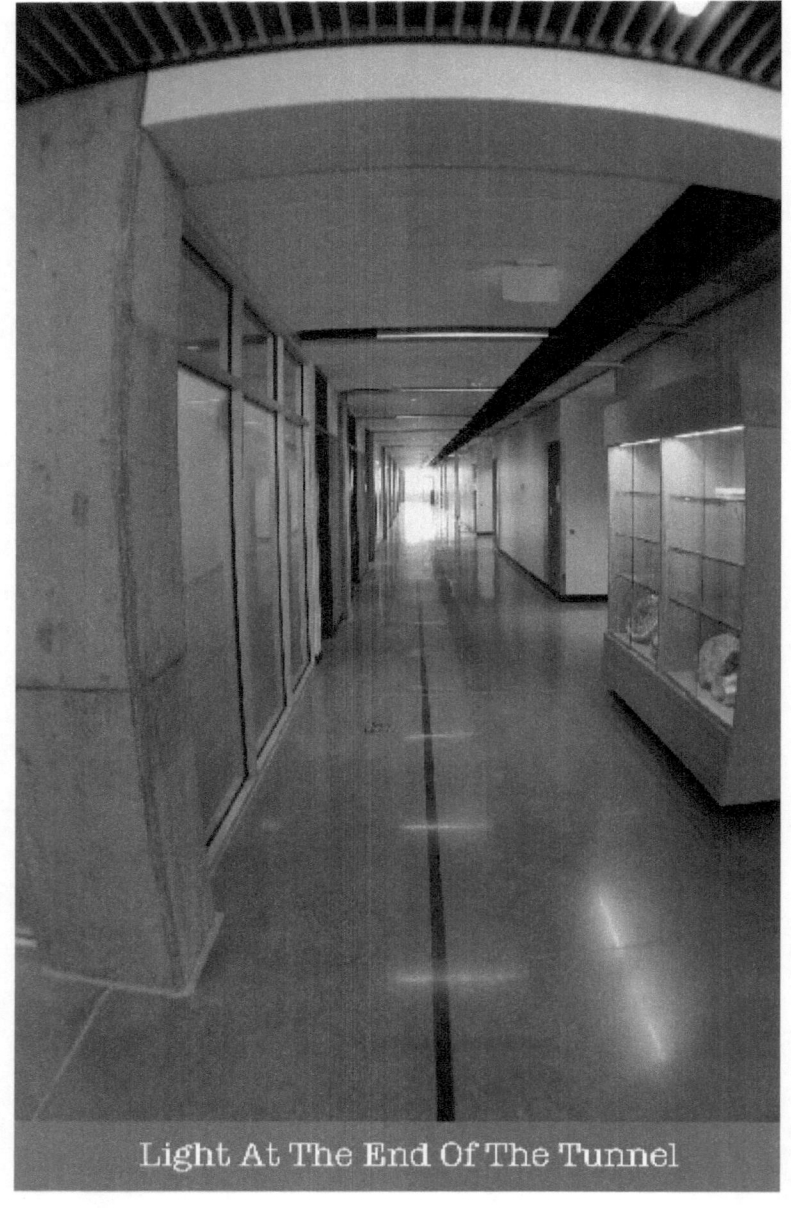
Light At The End Of The Tunnel

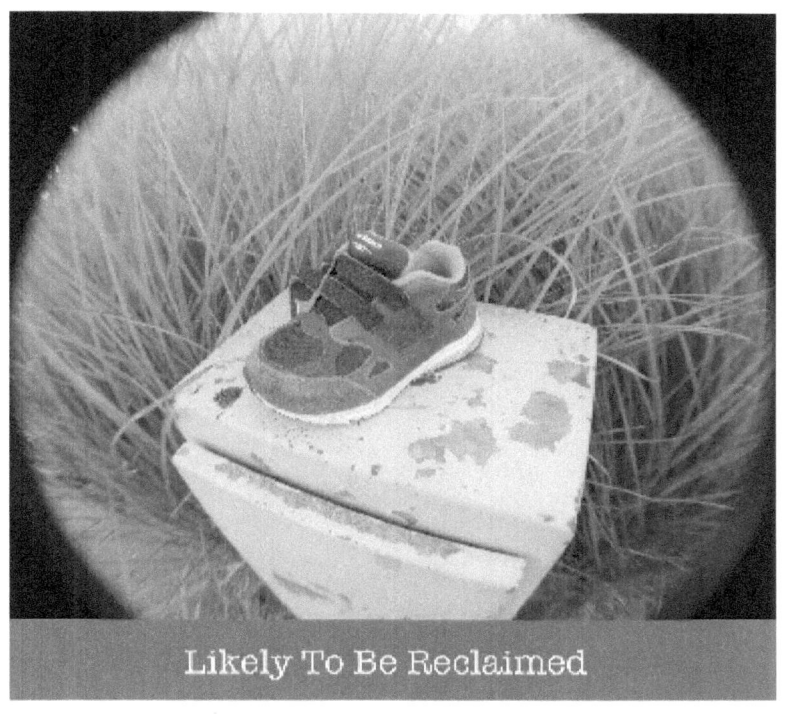

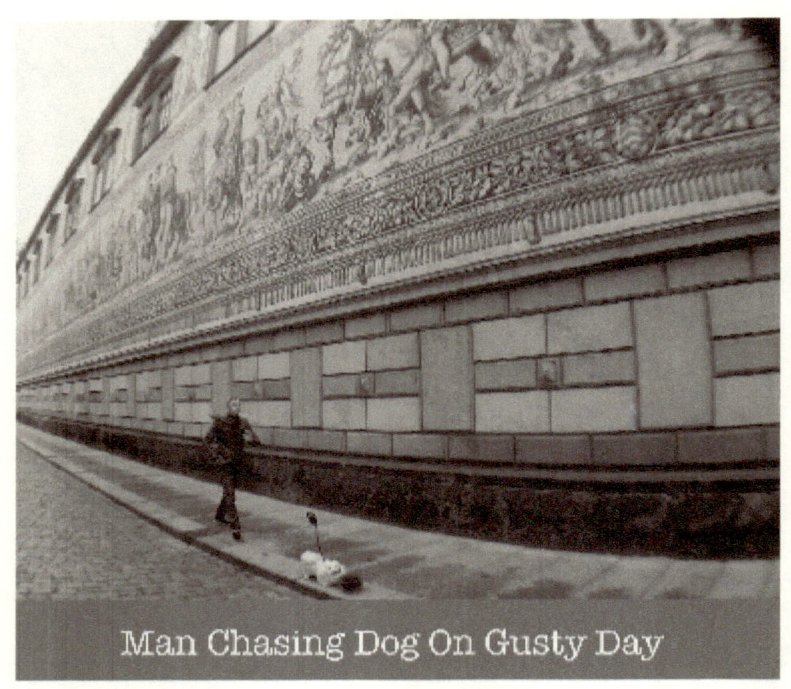

Man Chasing Dog On Gusty Day

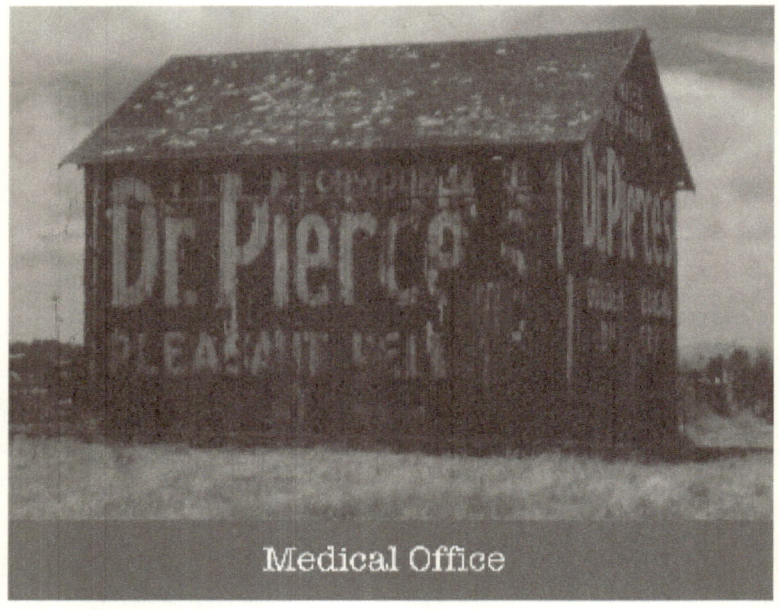

Medical Office

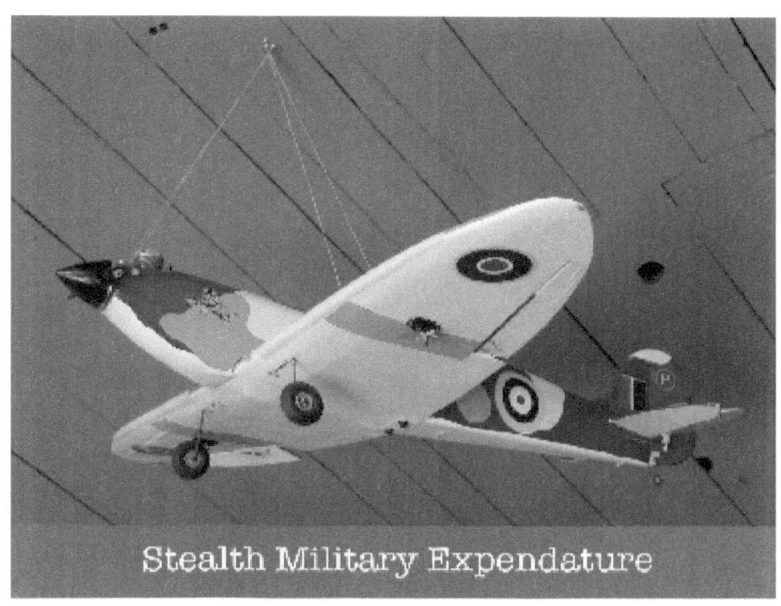

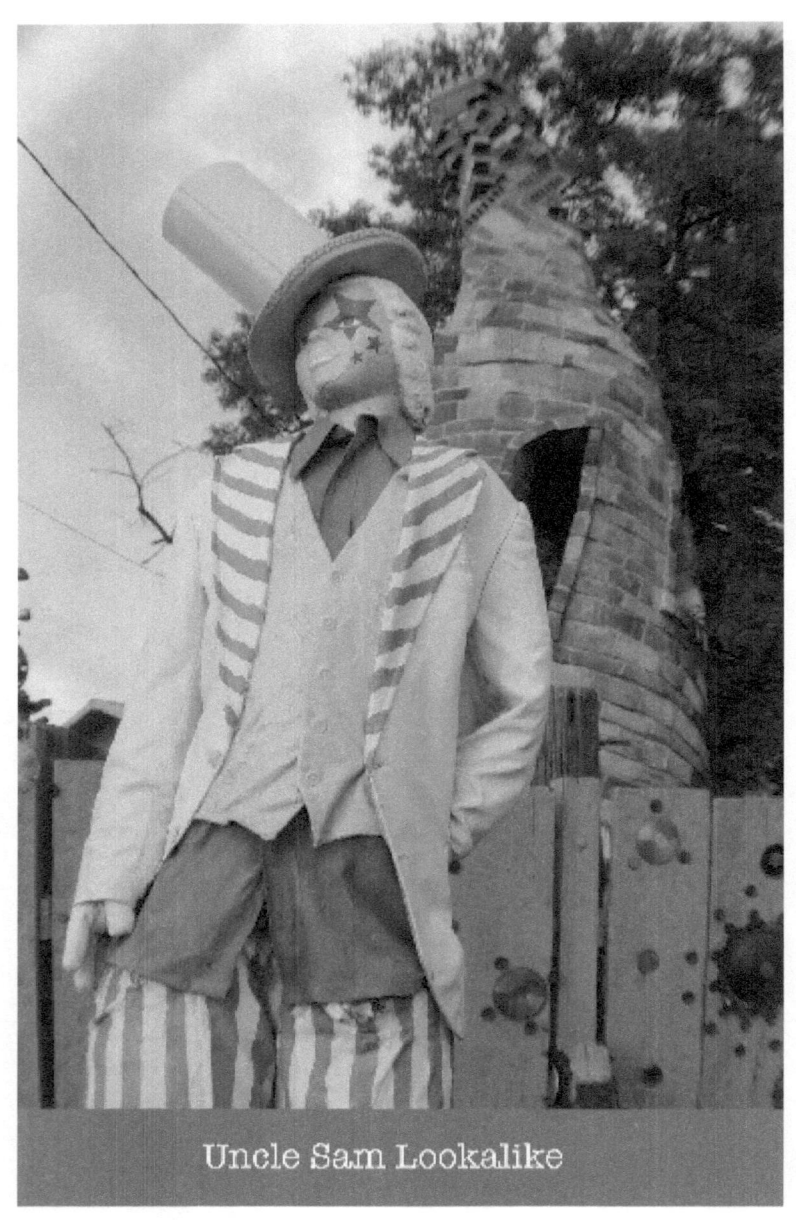

Uncle Sam Lookalike

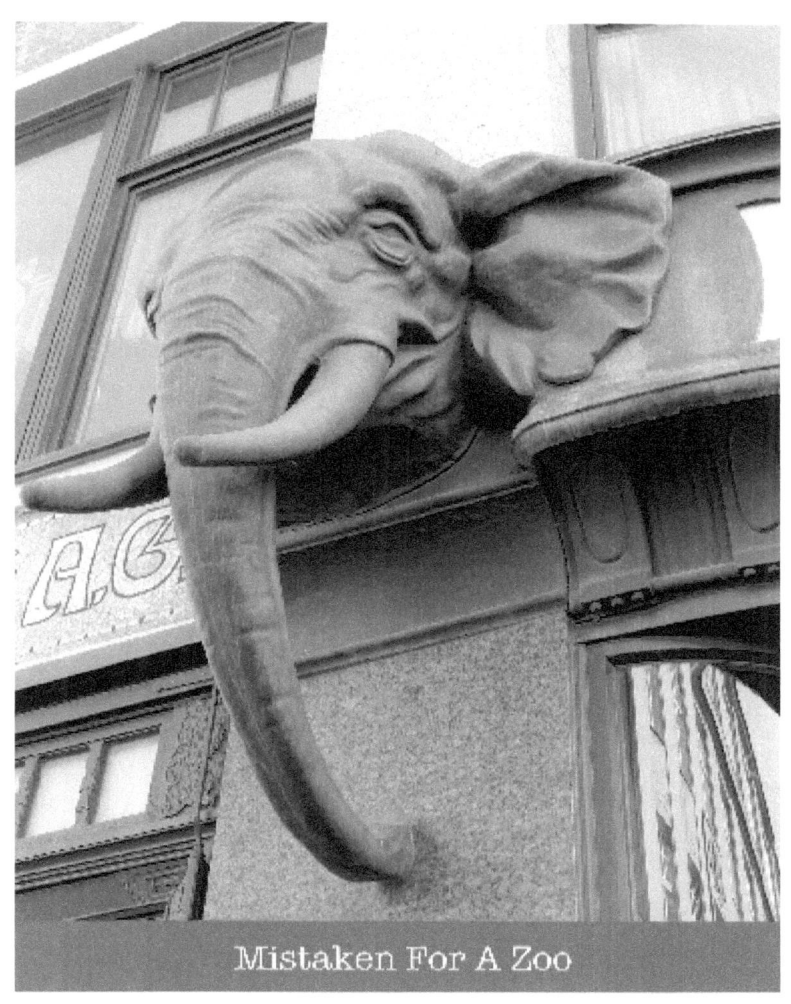
Mistaken For A Zoo

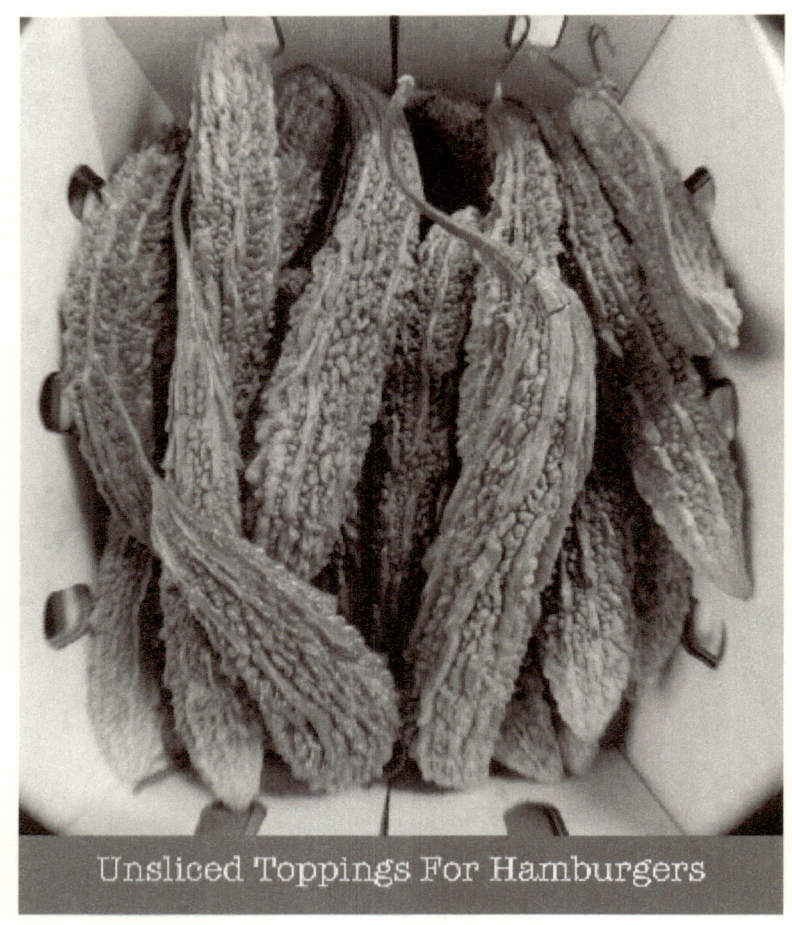

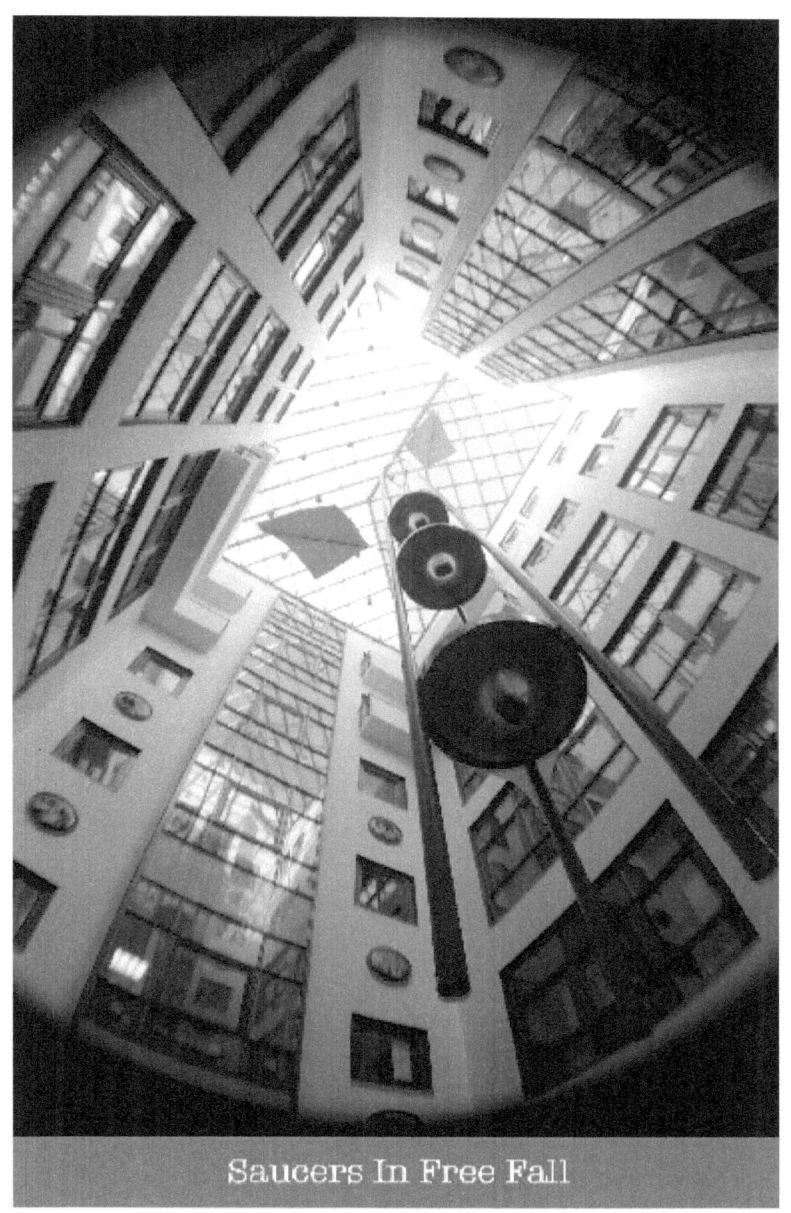

Saucers In Free Fall

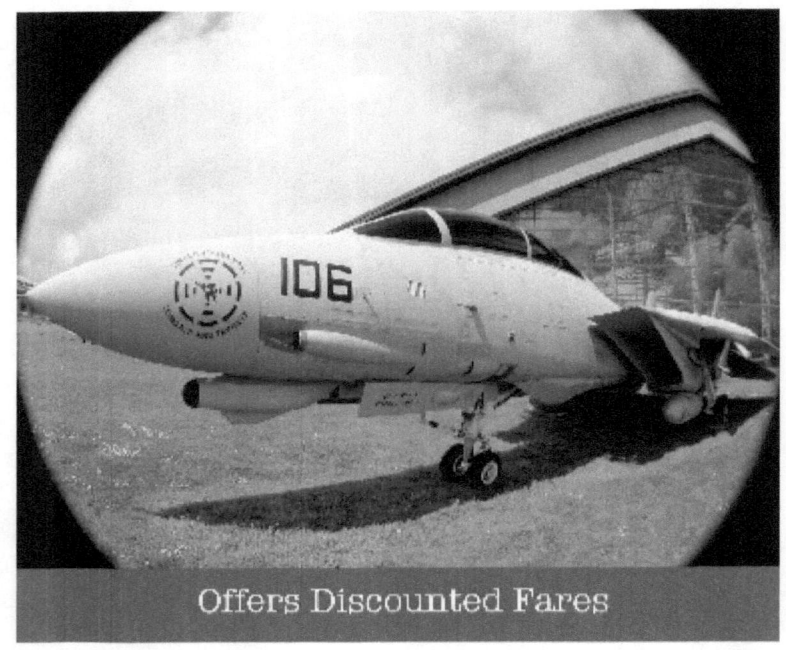
Offers Discounted Fares

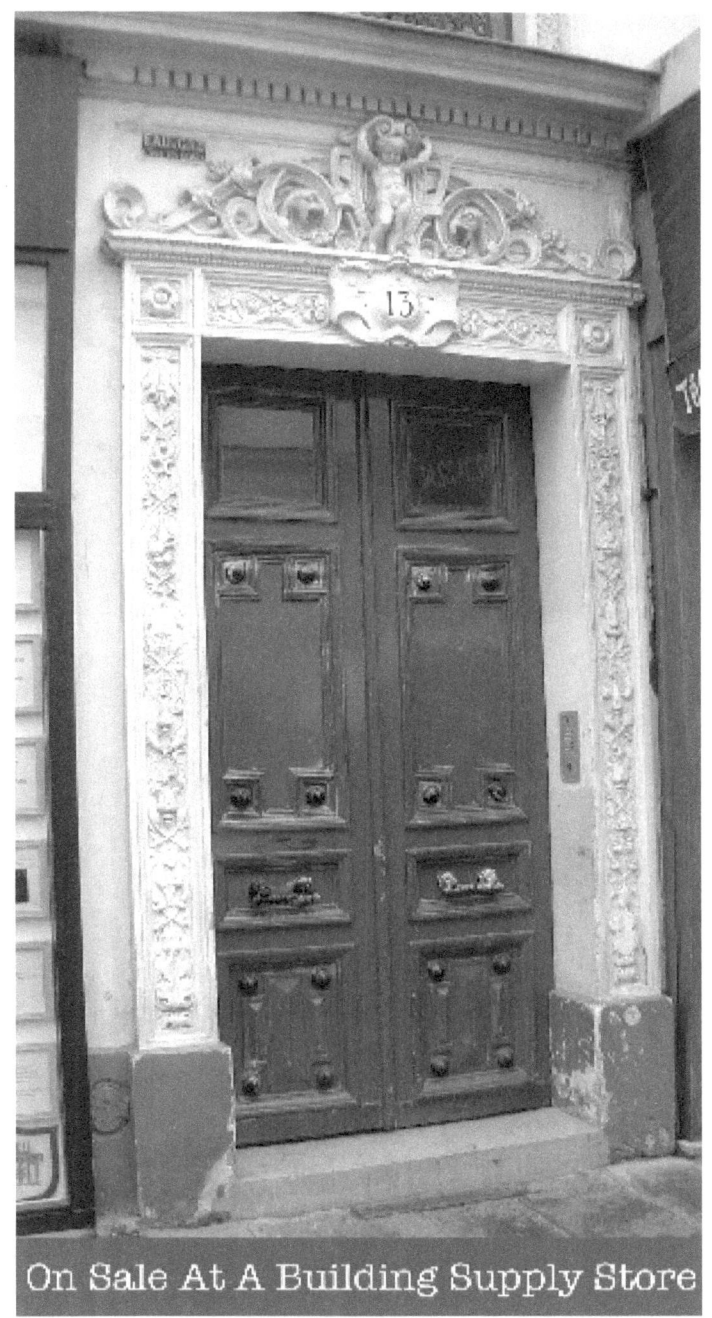

On Sale At A Building Supply Store

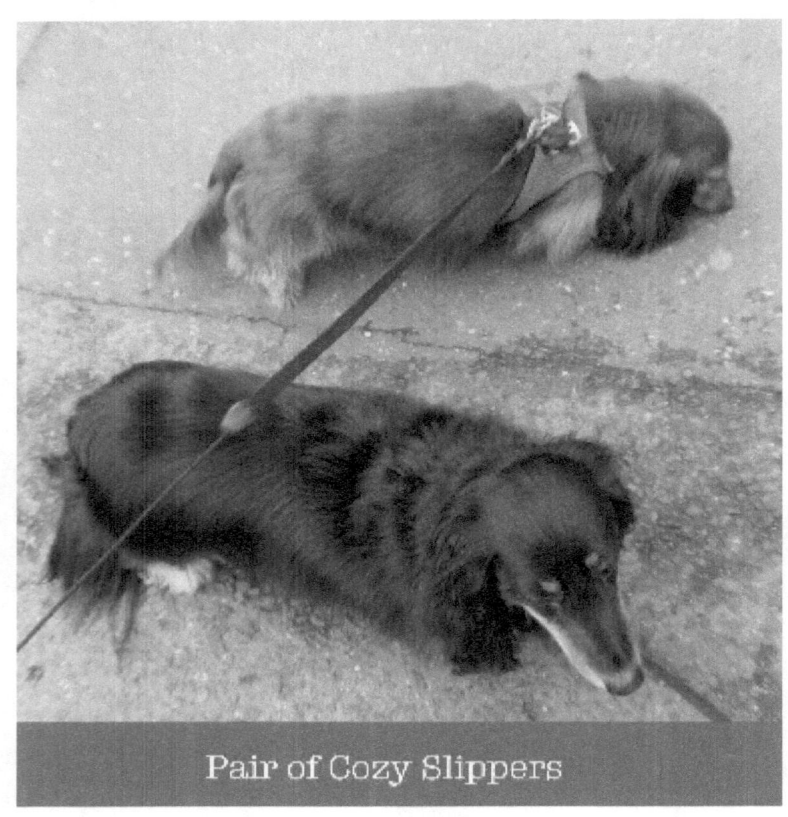

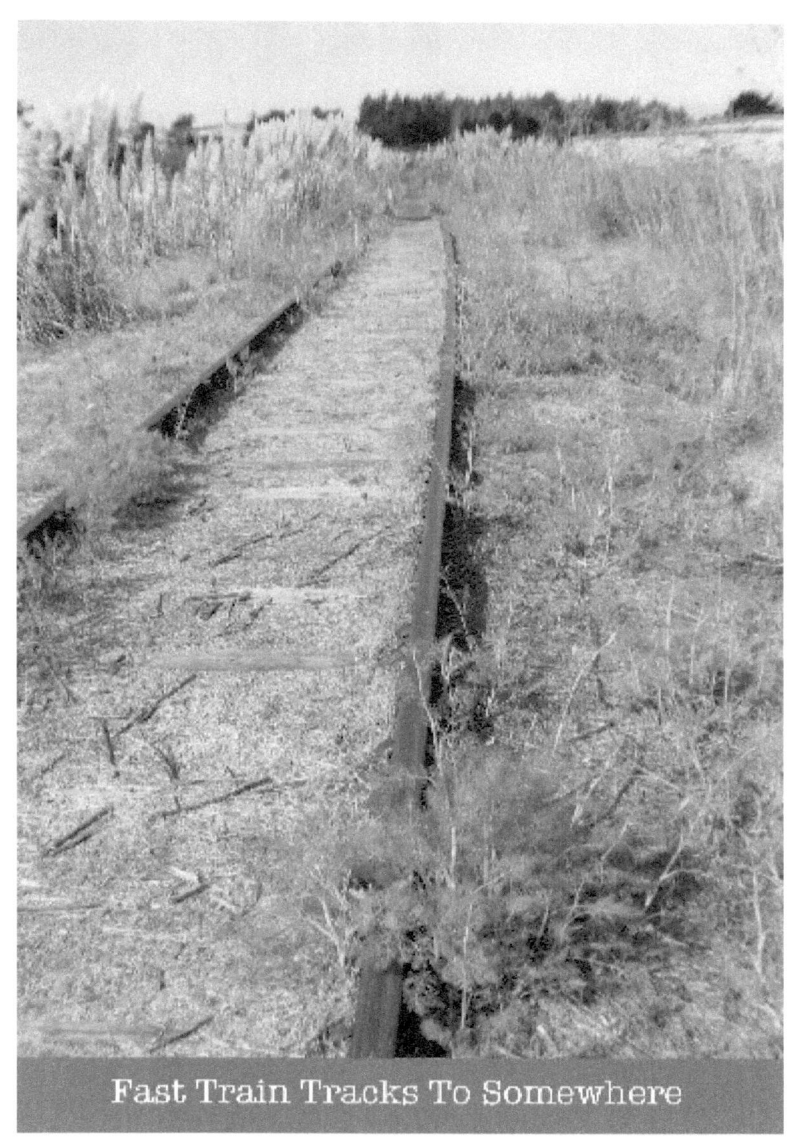

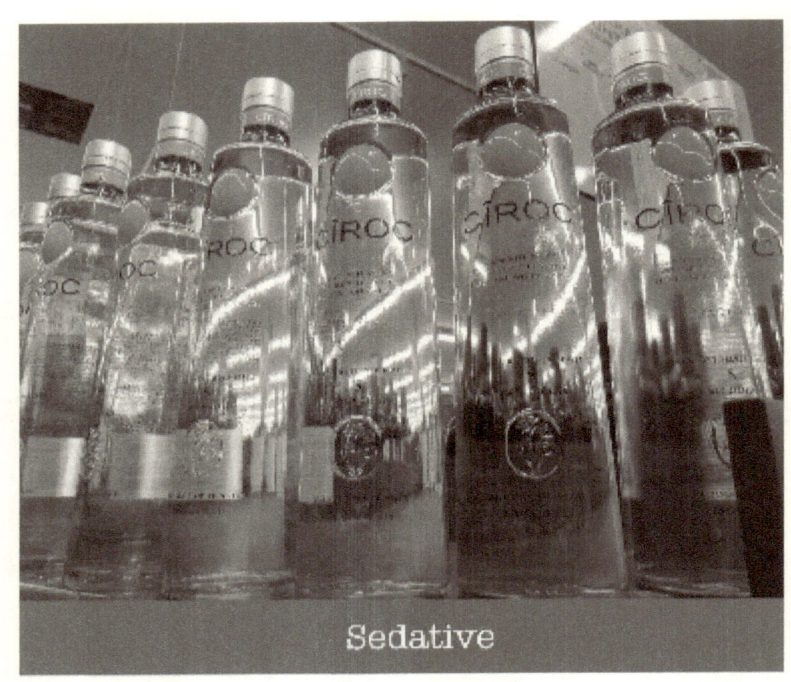
Sedative

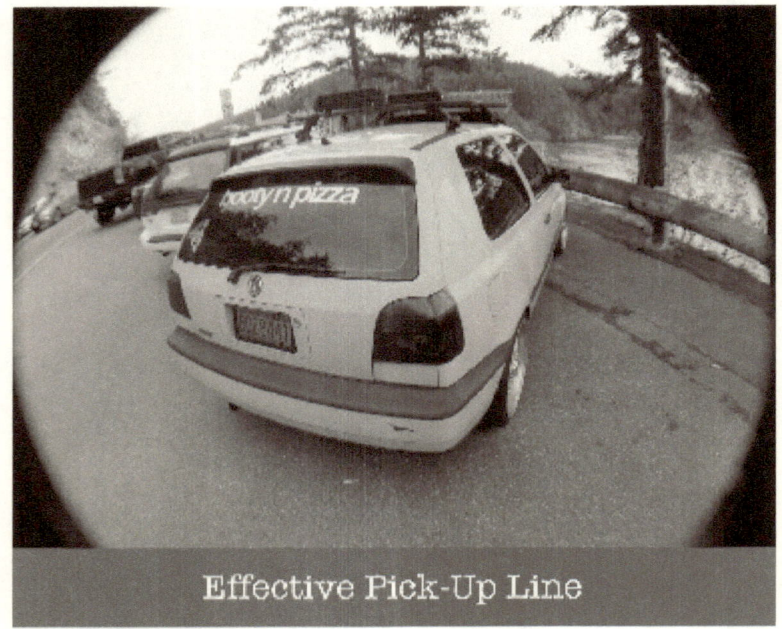
Effective Pick-Up Line

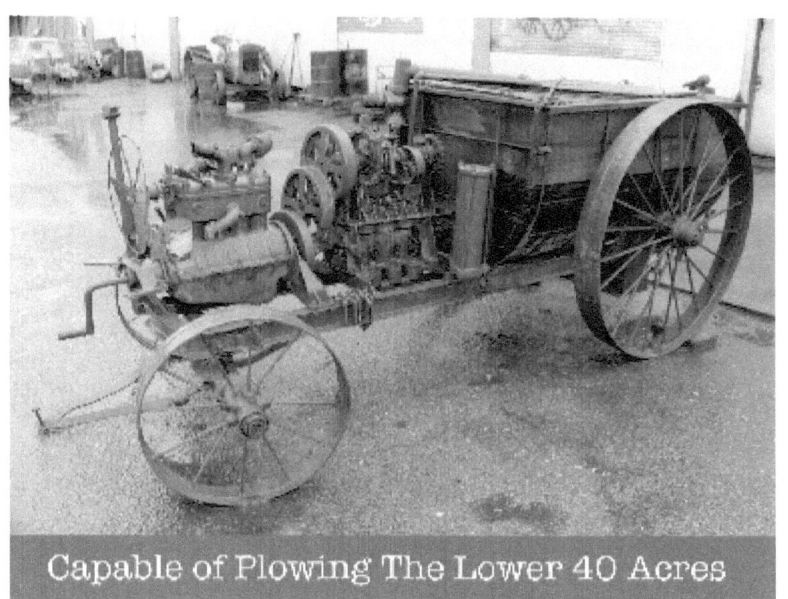
Capable of Plowing The Lower 40 Acres

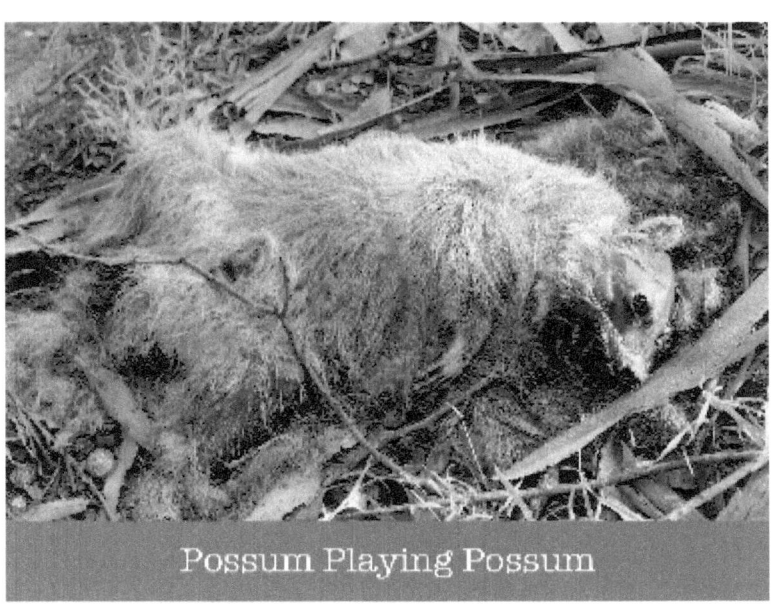
Possum Playing Possum

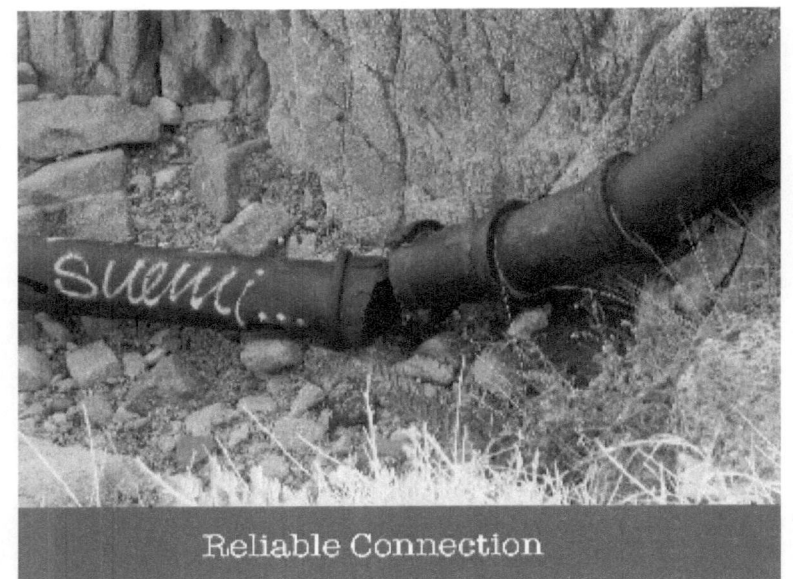
Reliable Connection

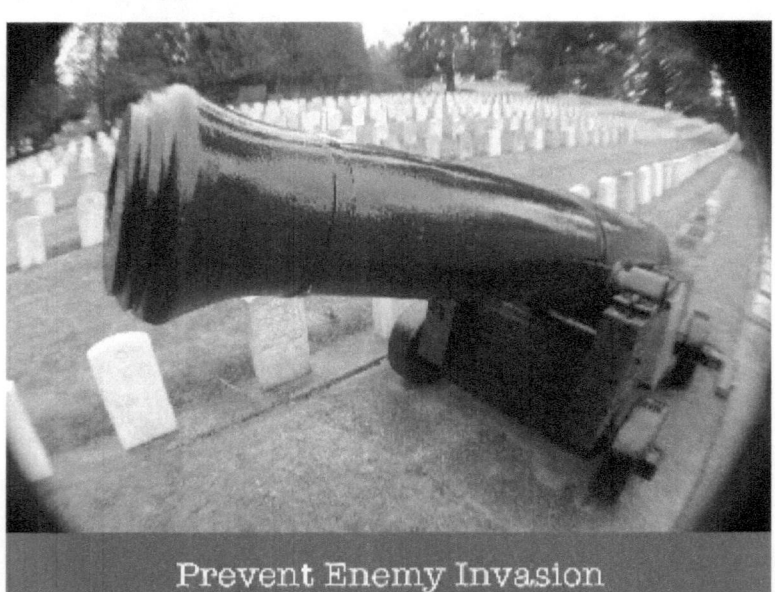
Prevent Enemy Invasion

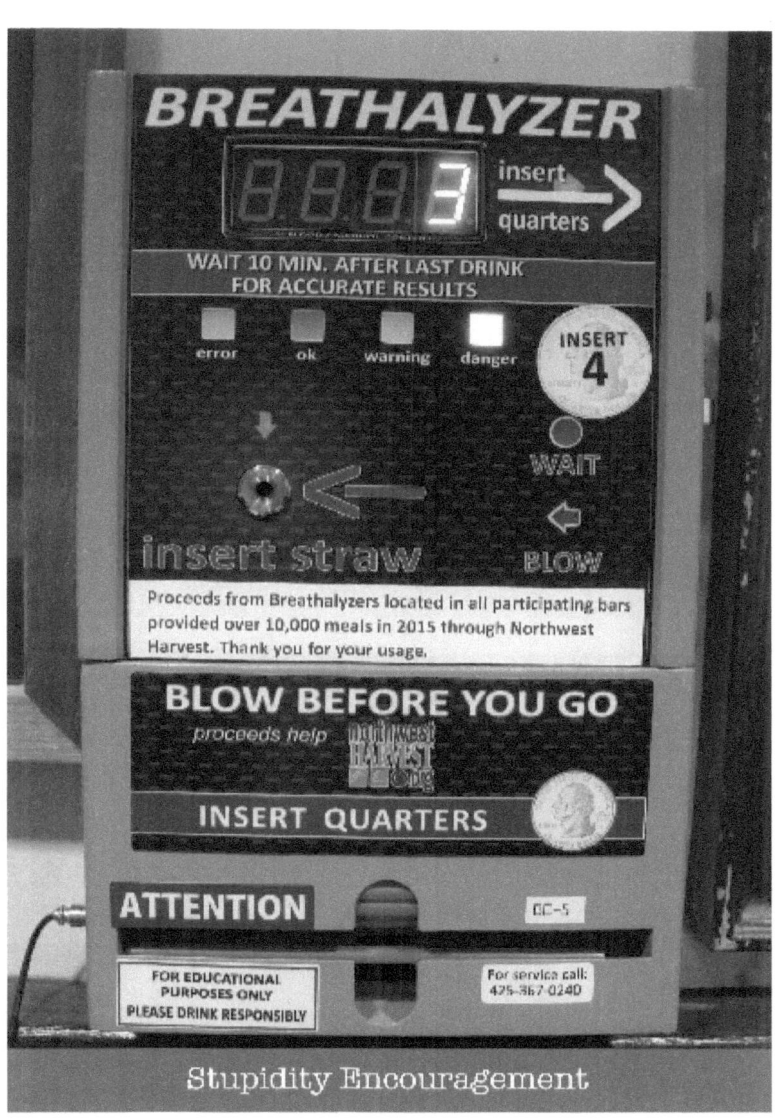

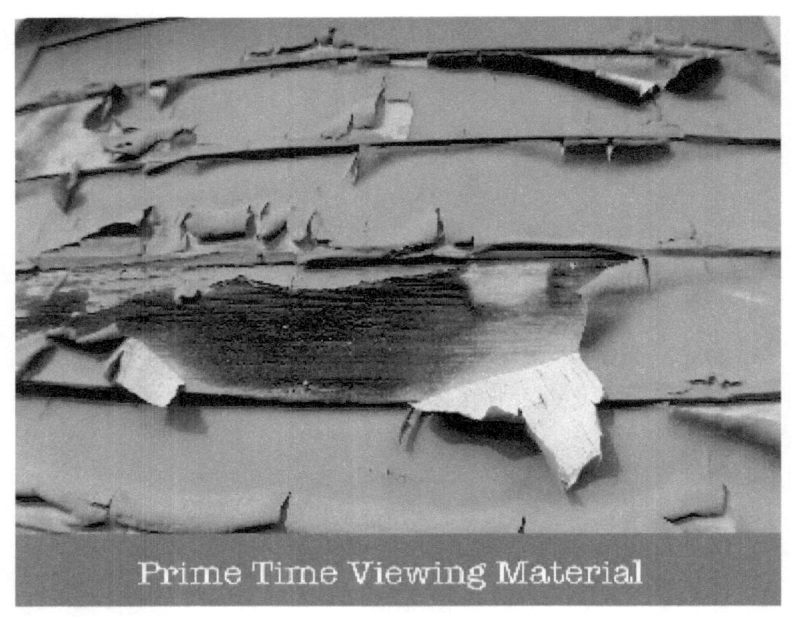
Prime Time Viewing Material

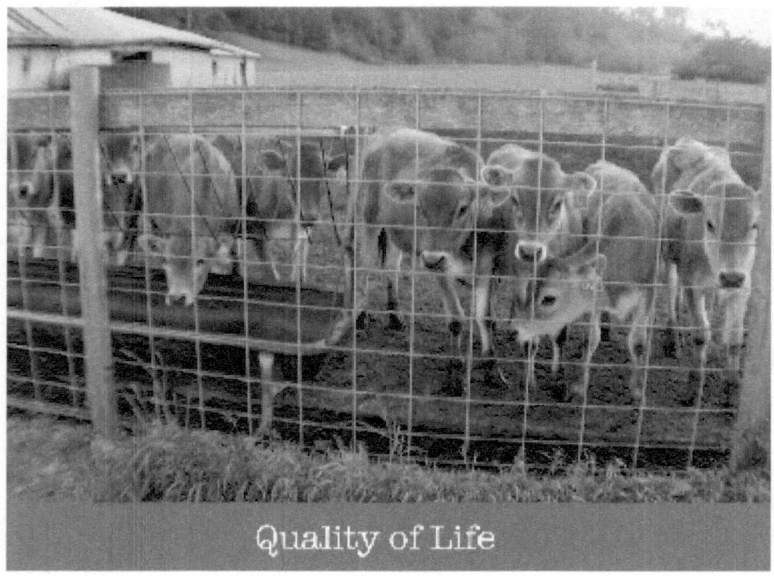
Quality of Life

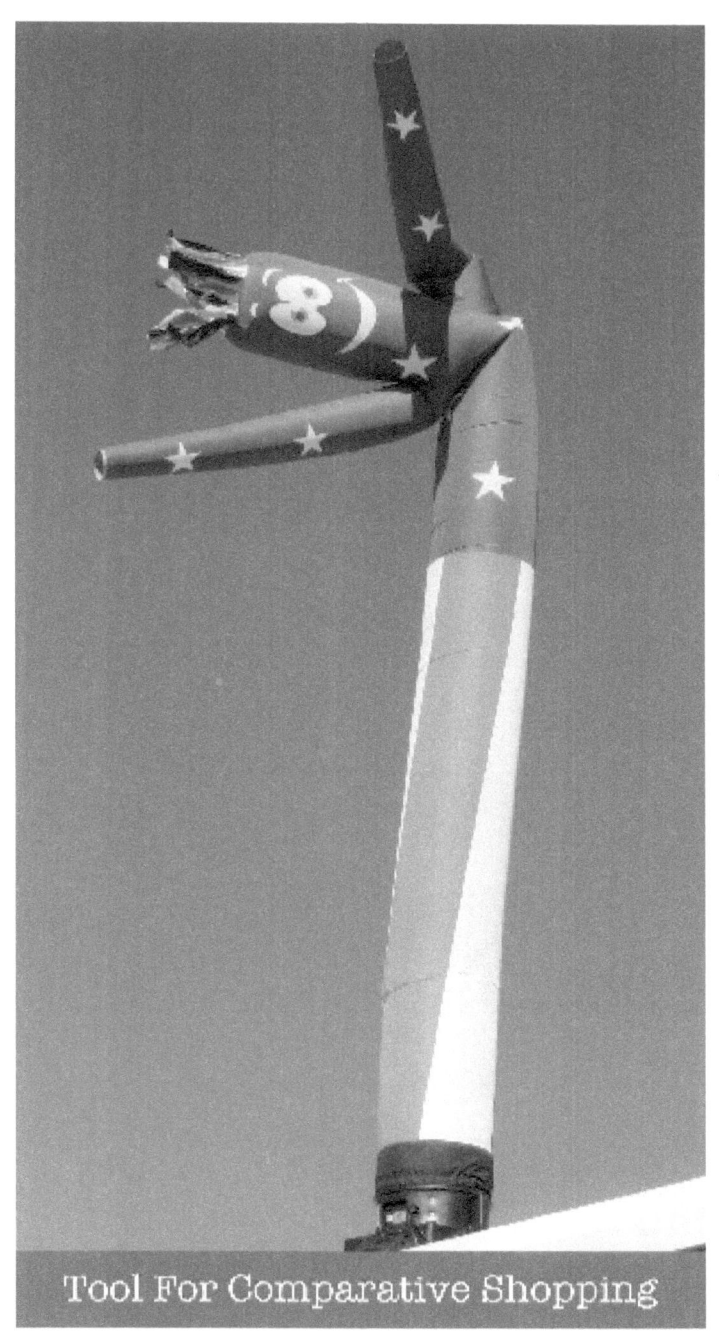
Tool For Comparative Shopping

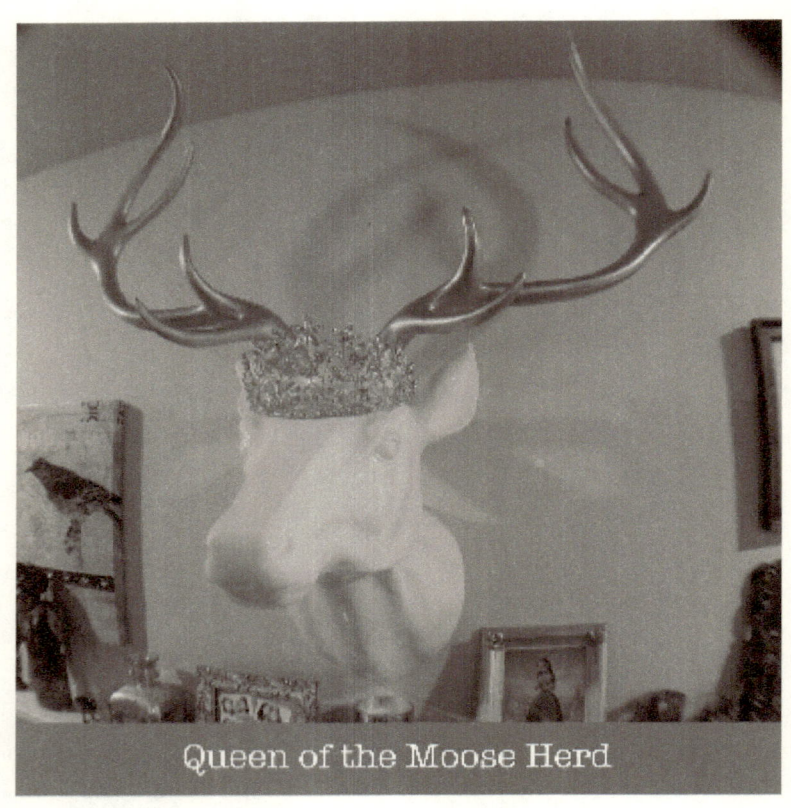

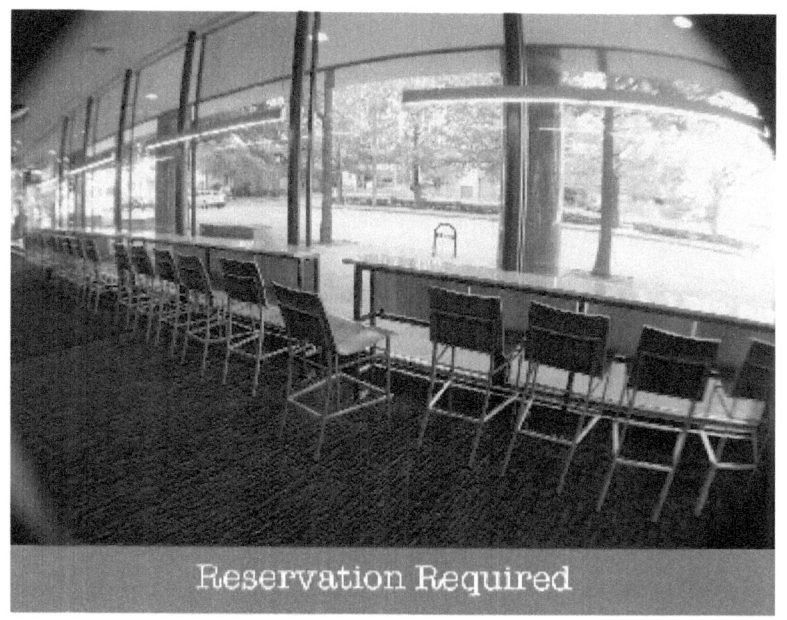

Reservation Required

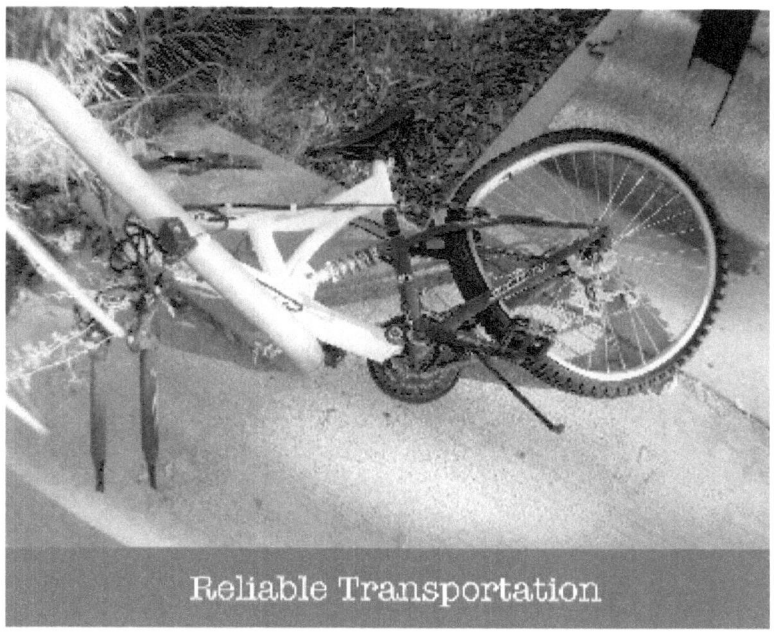

Reliable Transportation

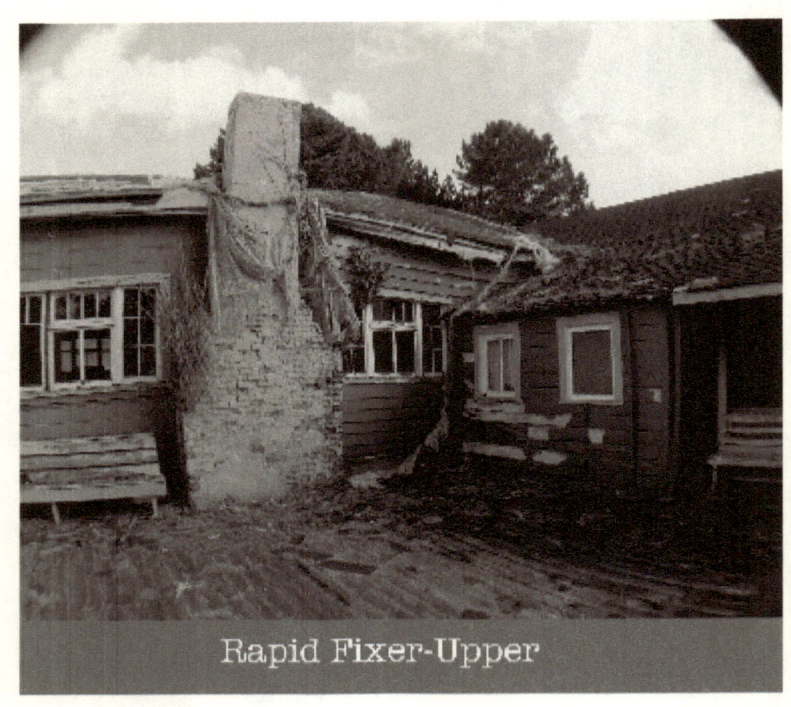
Rapid Fixer-Upper

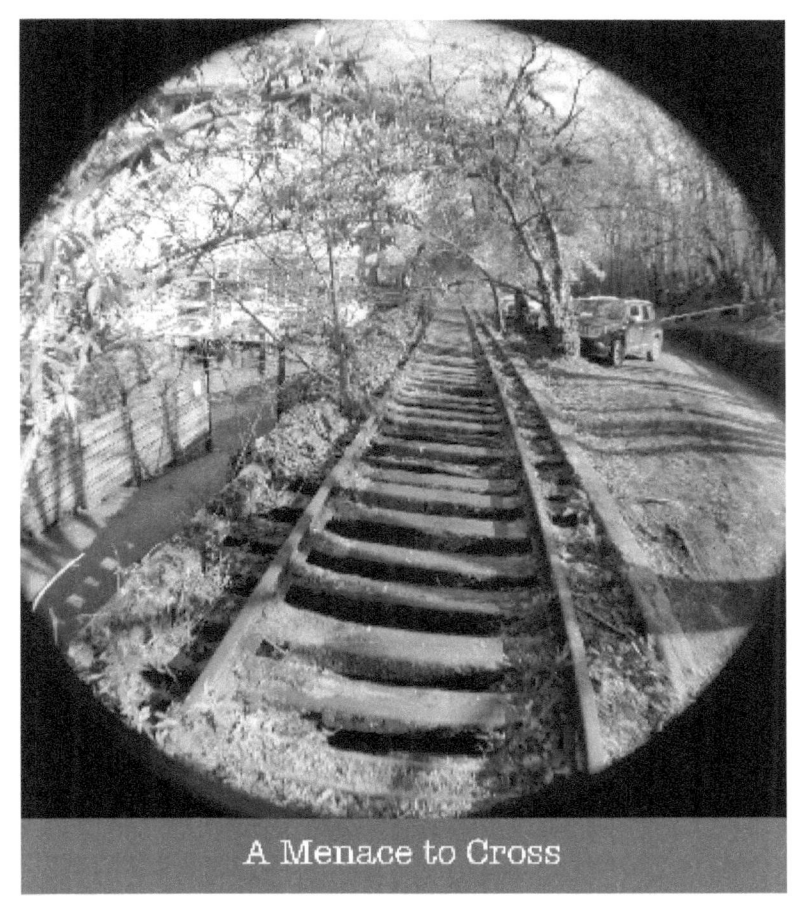

A Menace to Cross

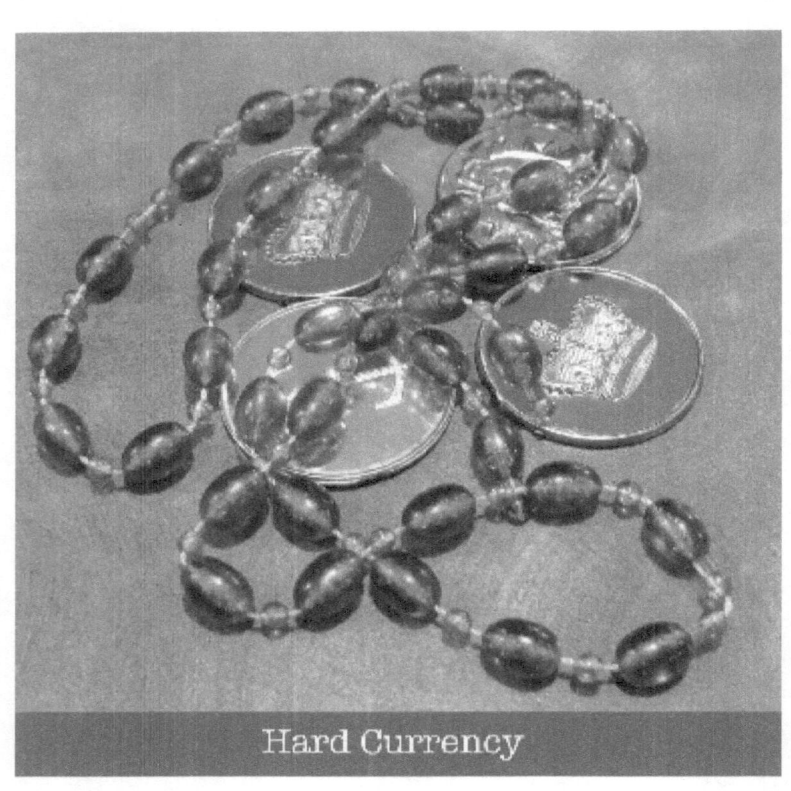

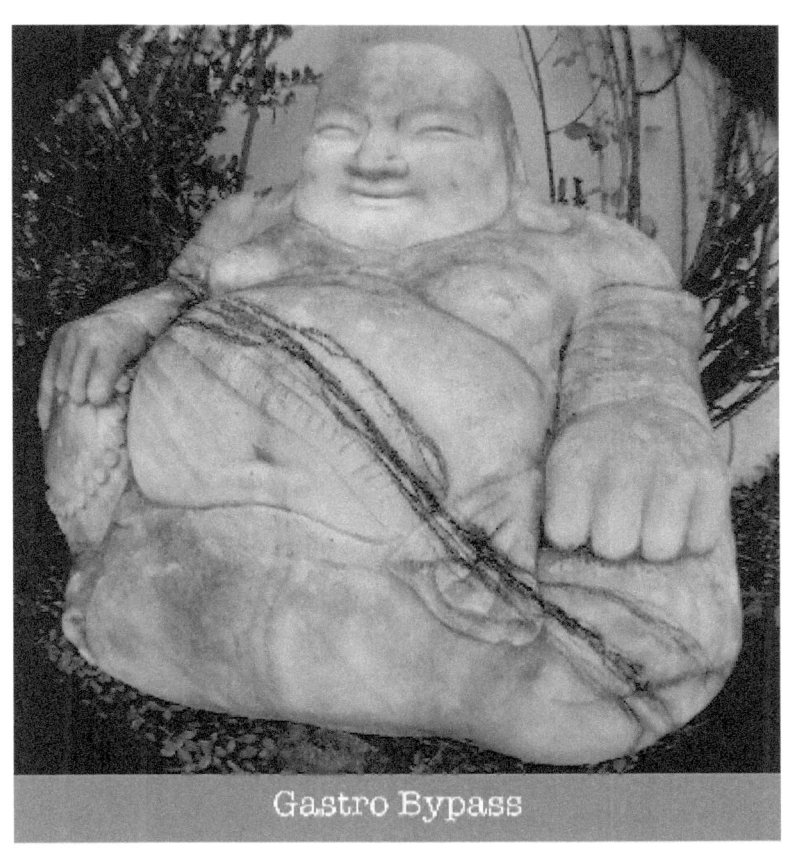
Gastro Bypass

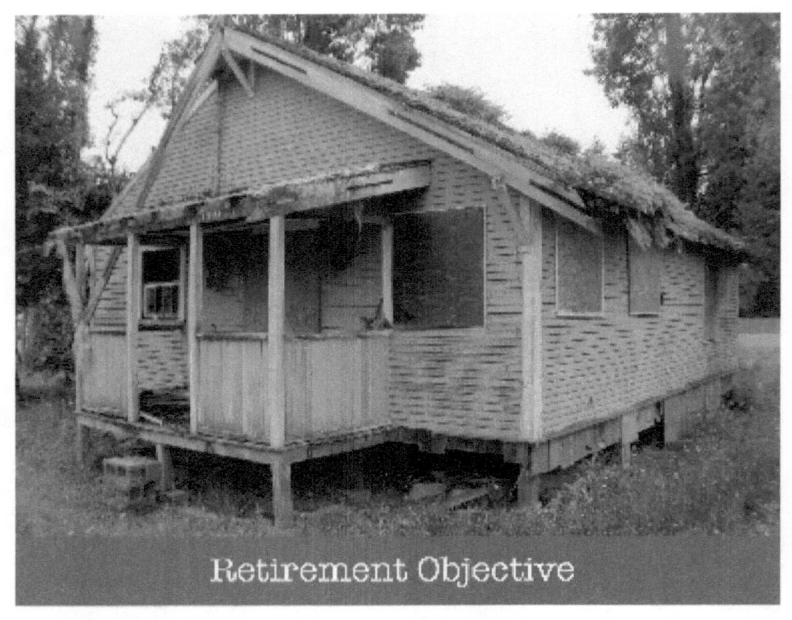
Retirement Objective

Romantic Literature

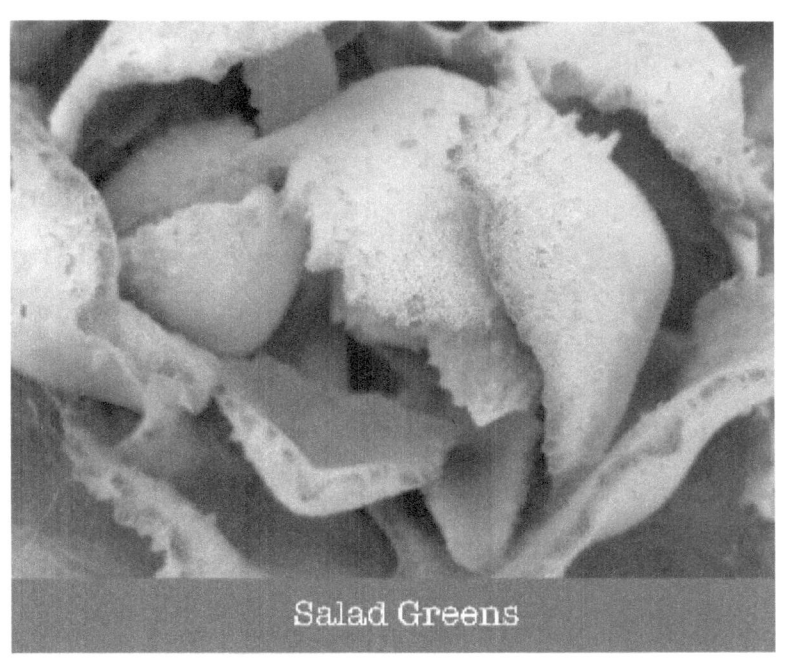

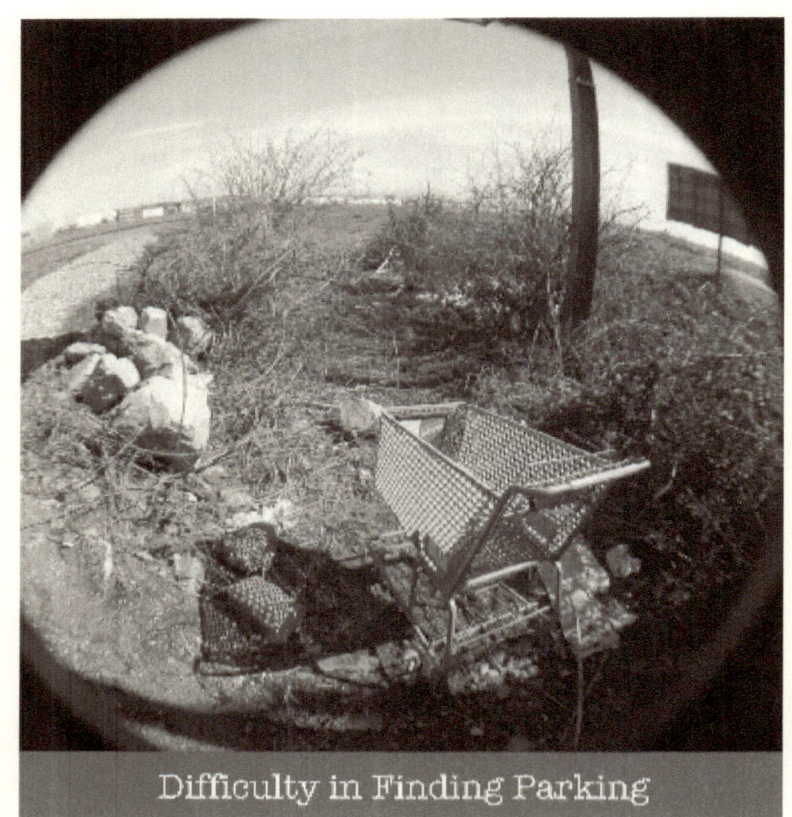
Difficulty in Finding Parking

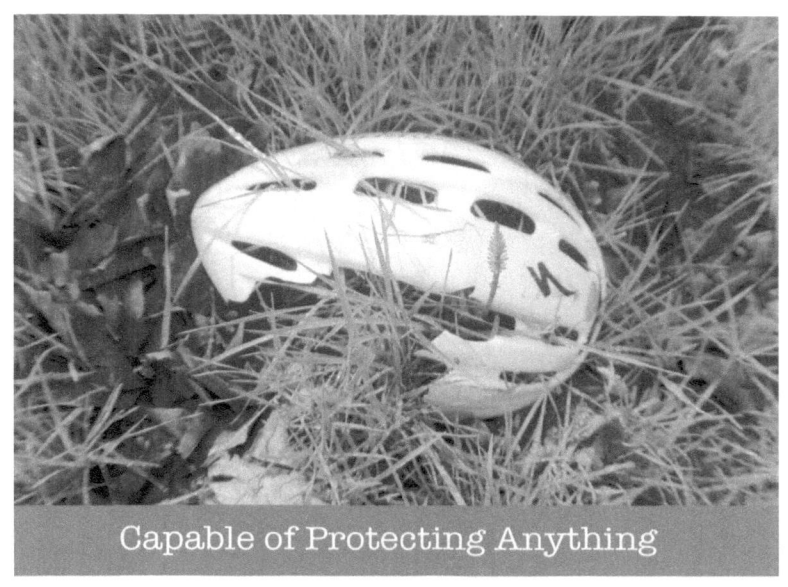
Capable of Protecting Anything

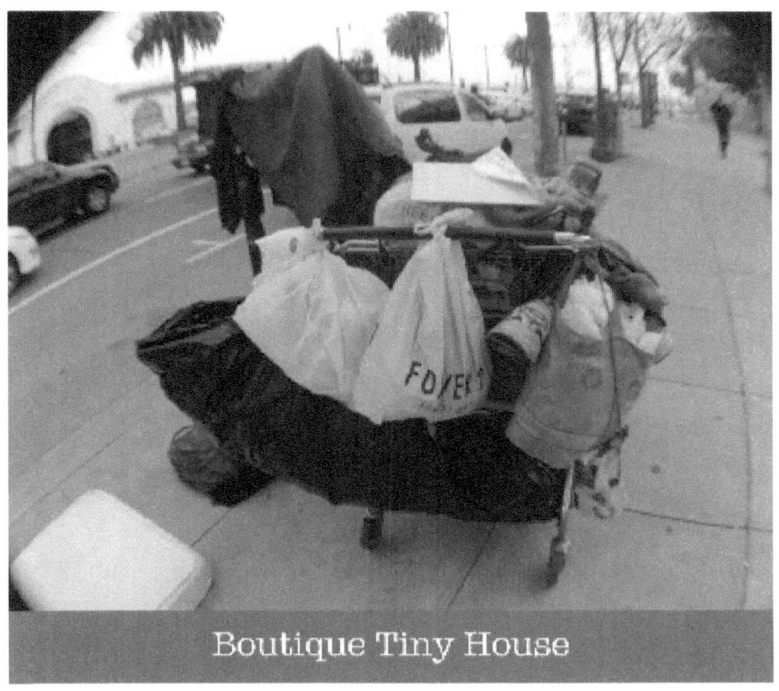
Boutique Tiny House

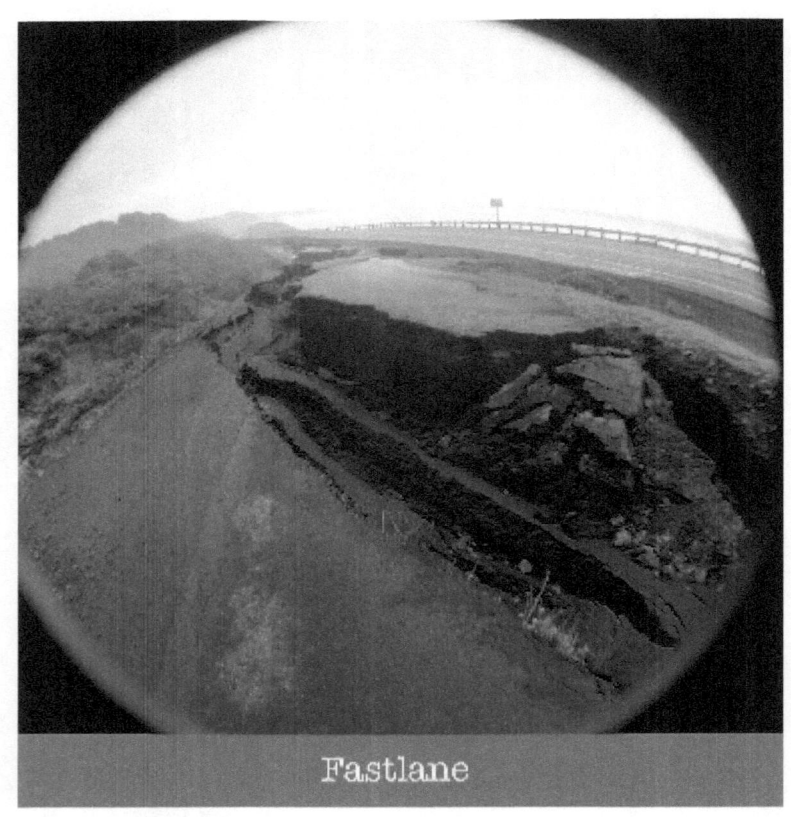

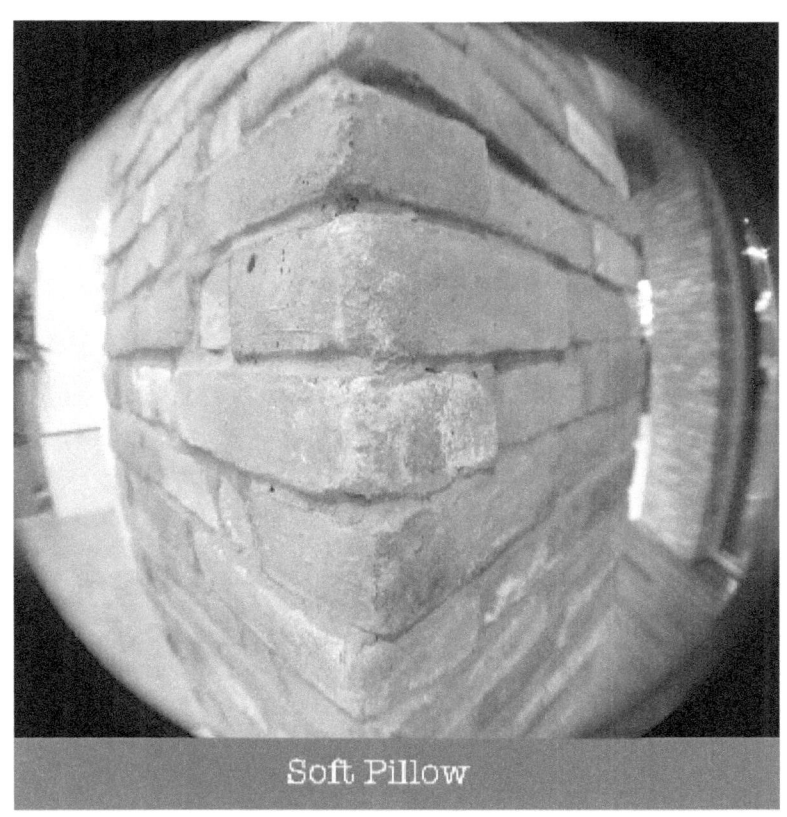

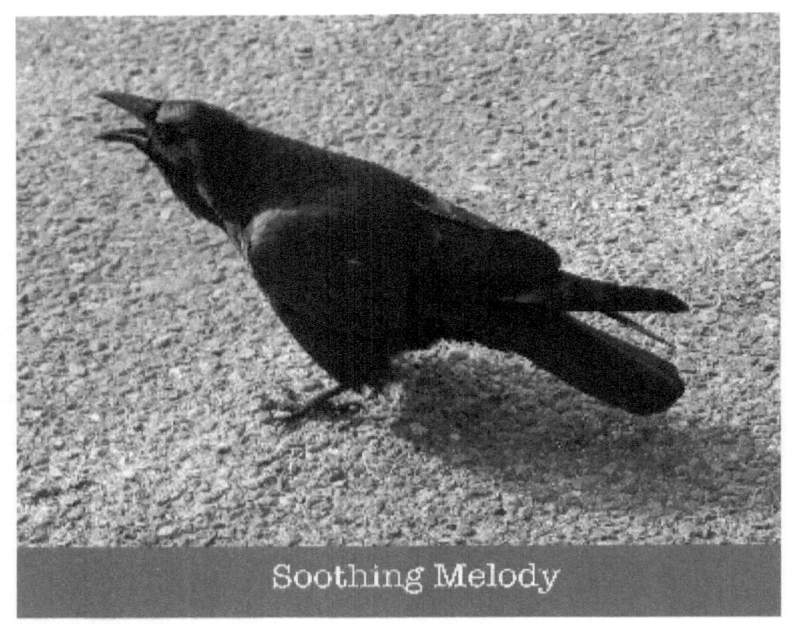
Soothing Melody

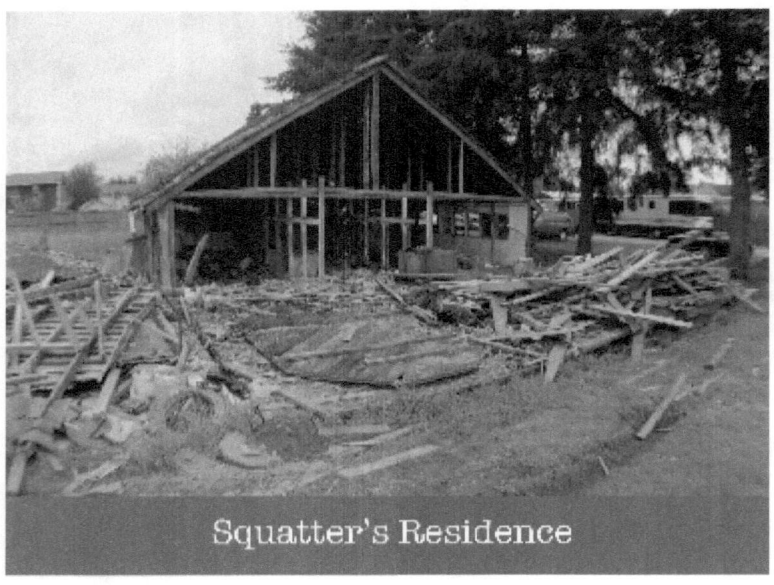
Squatter's Residence

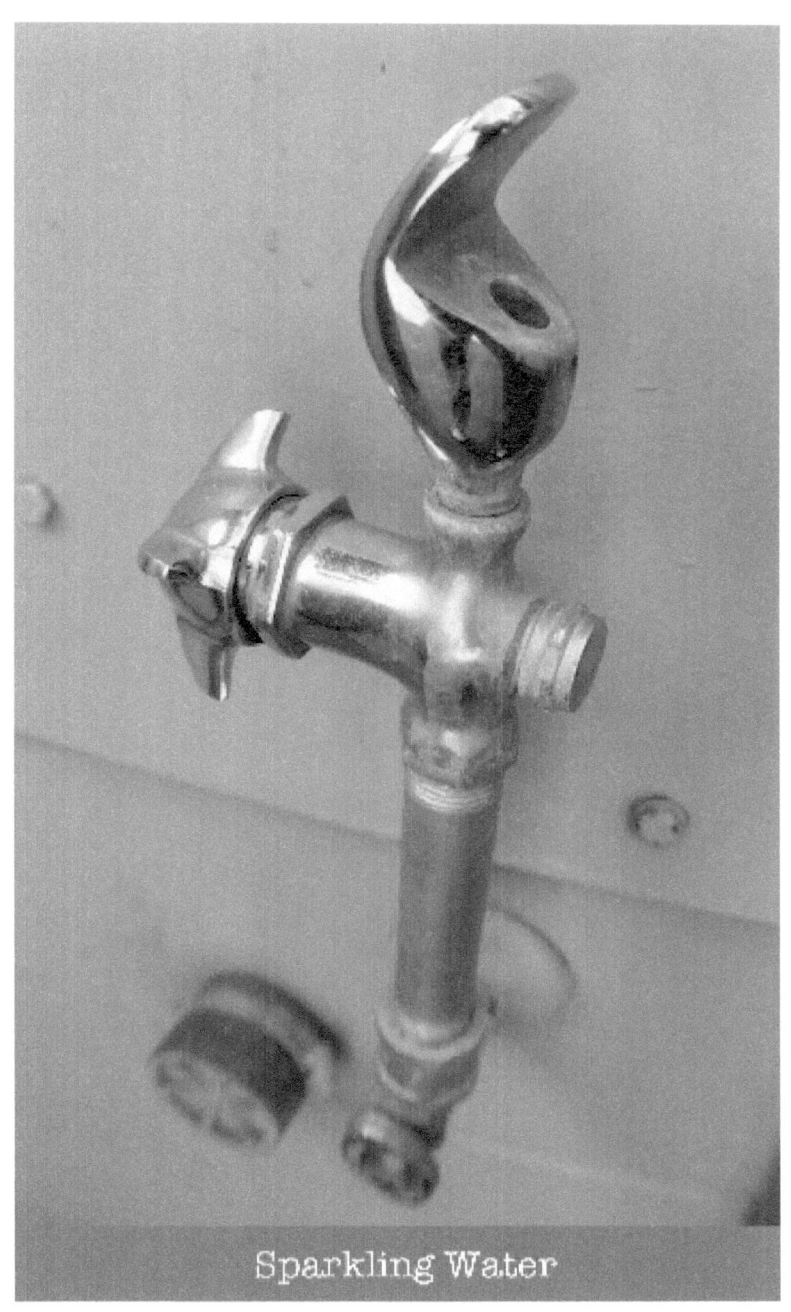

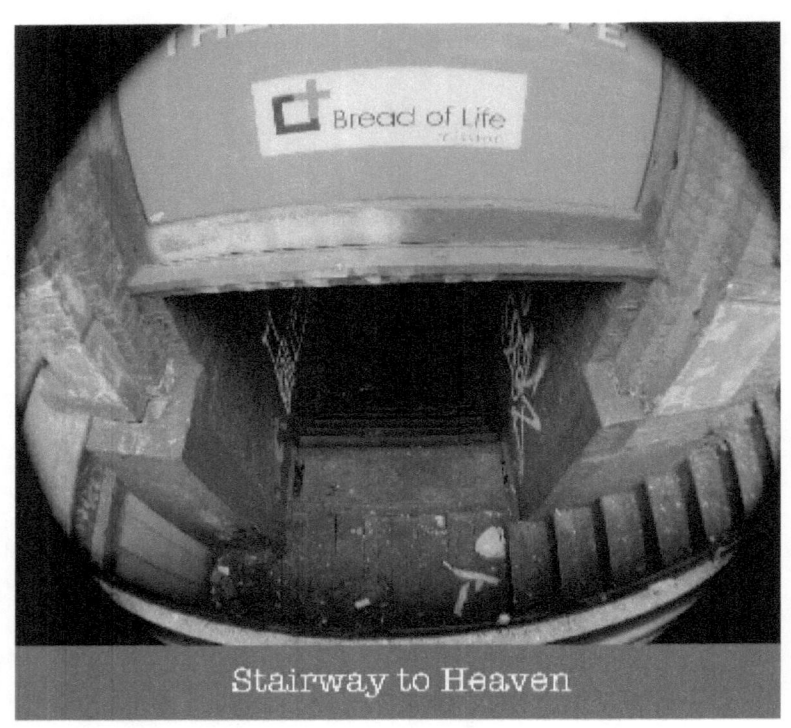

Stairway to Heaven

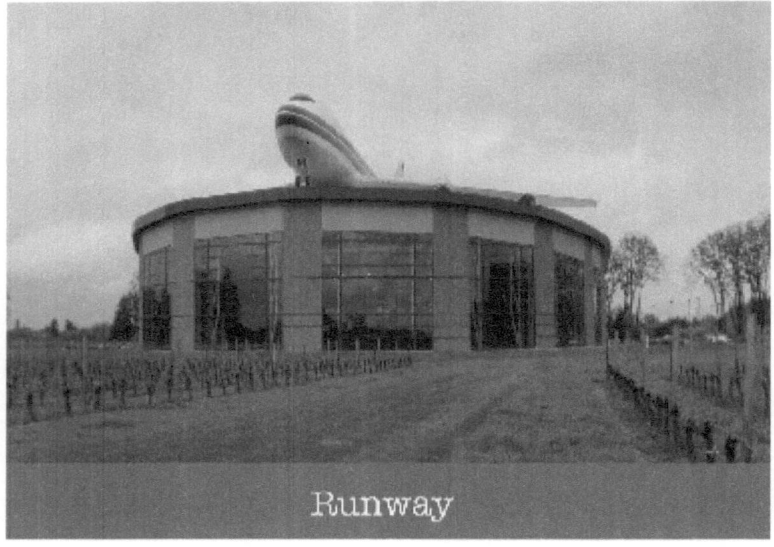

Runway

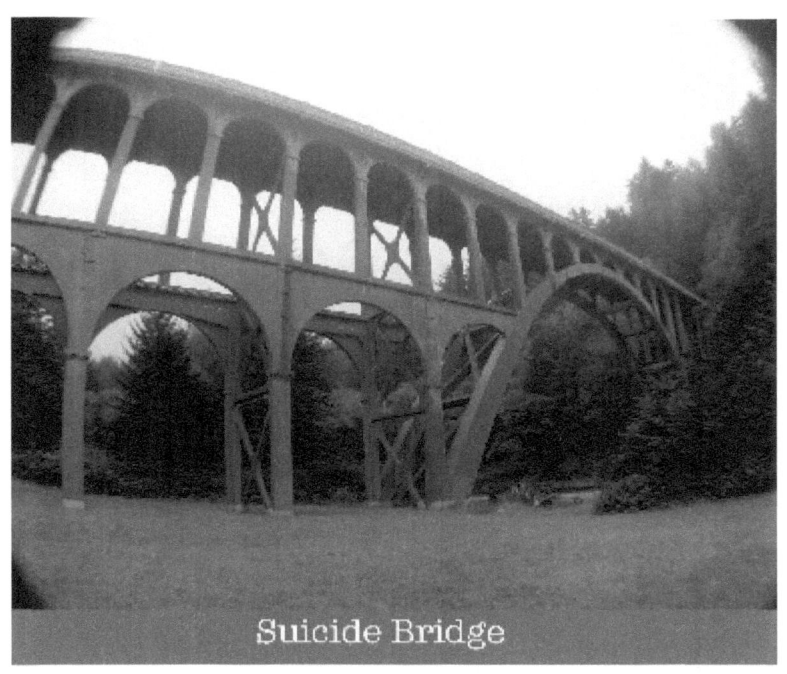

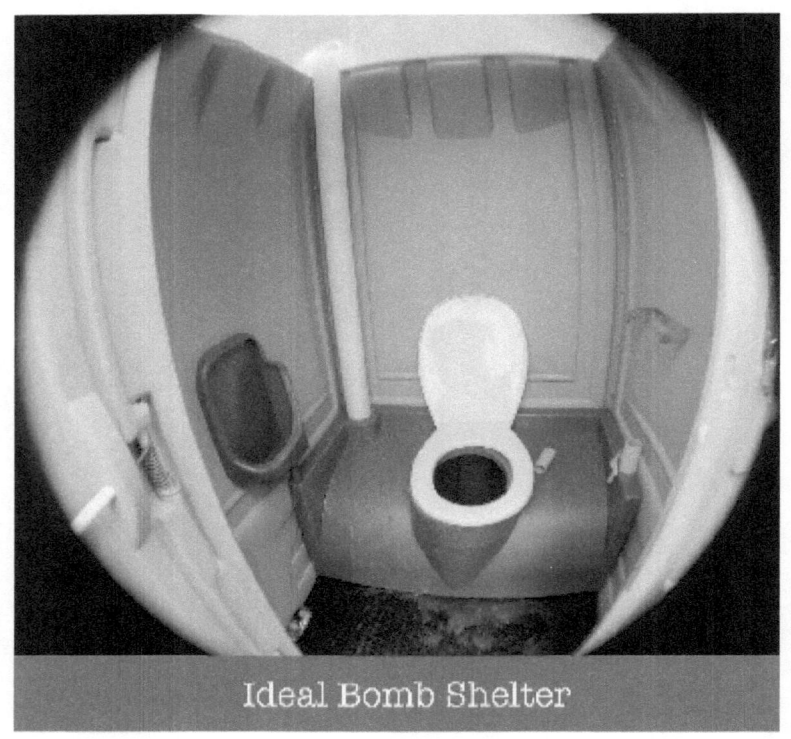

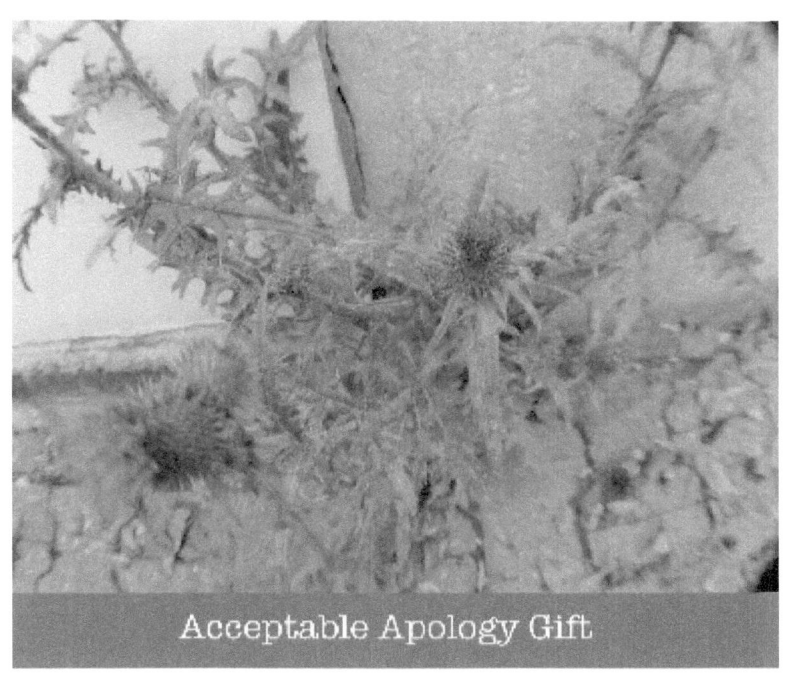

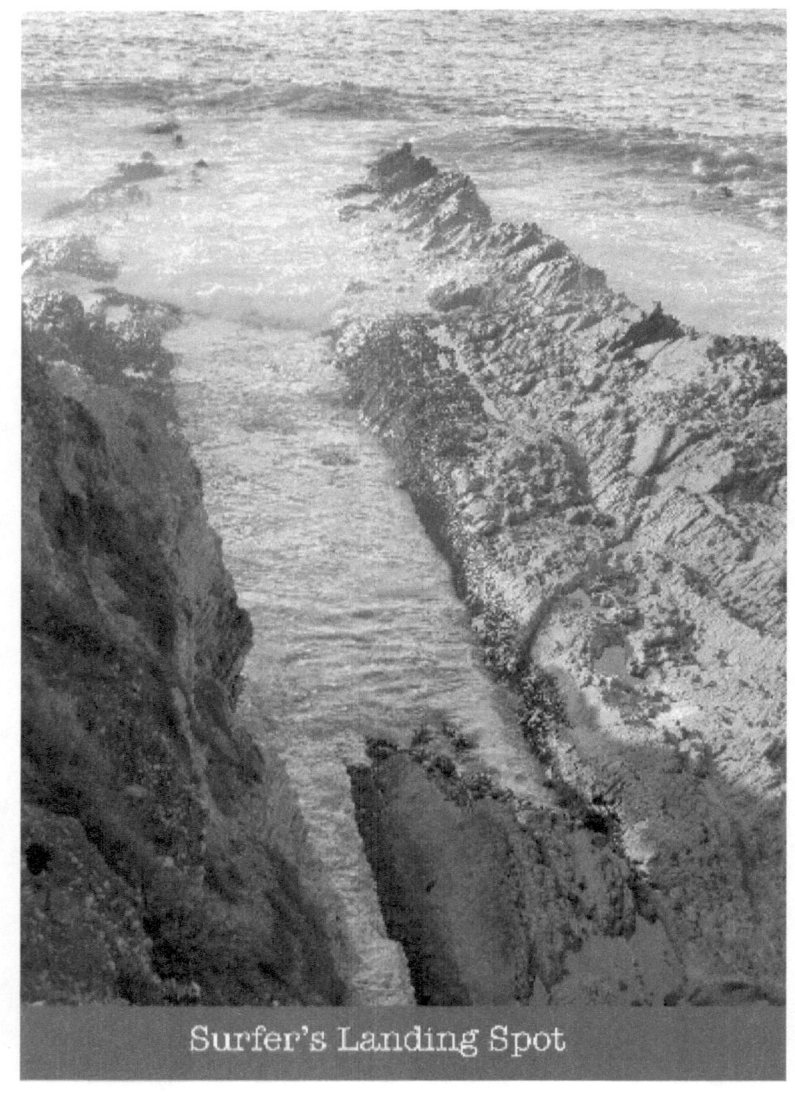
Surfer's Landing Spot

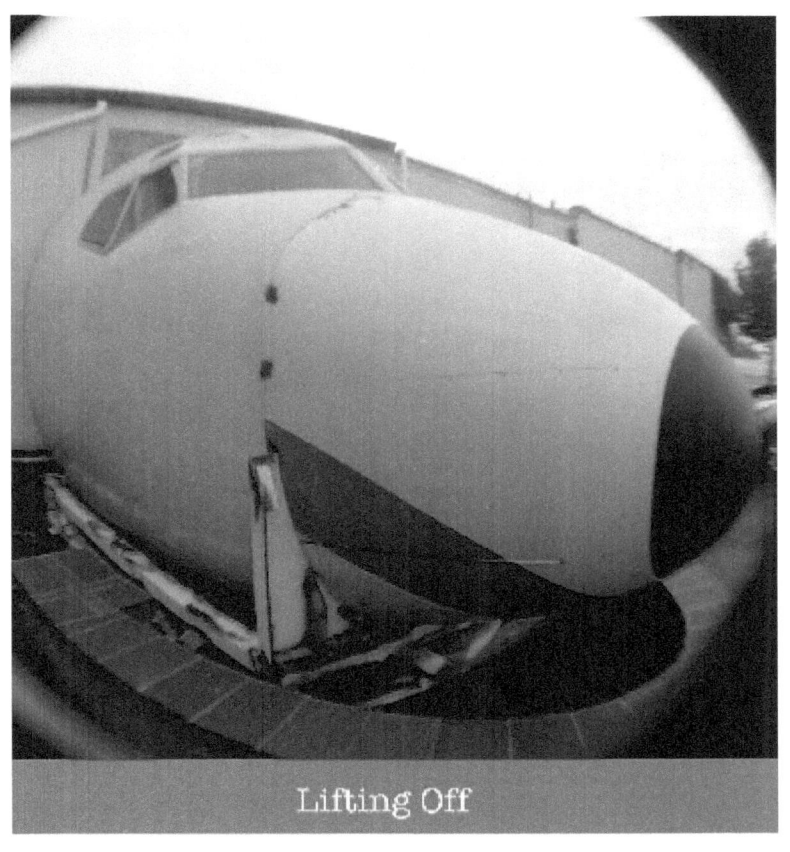

Lifting Off

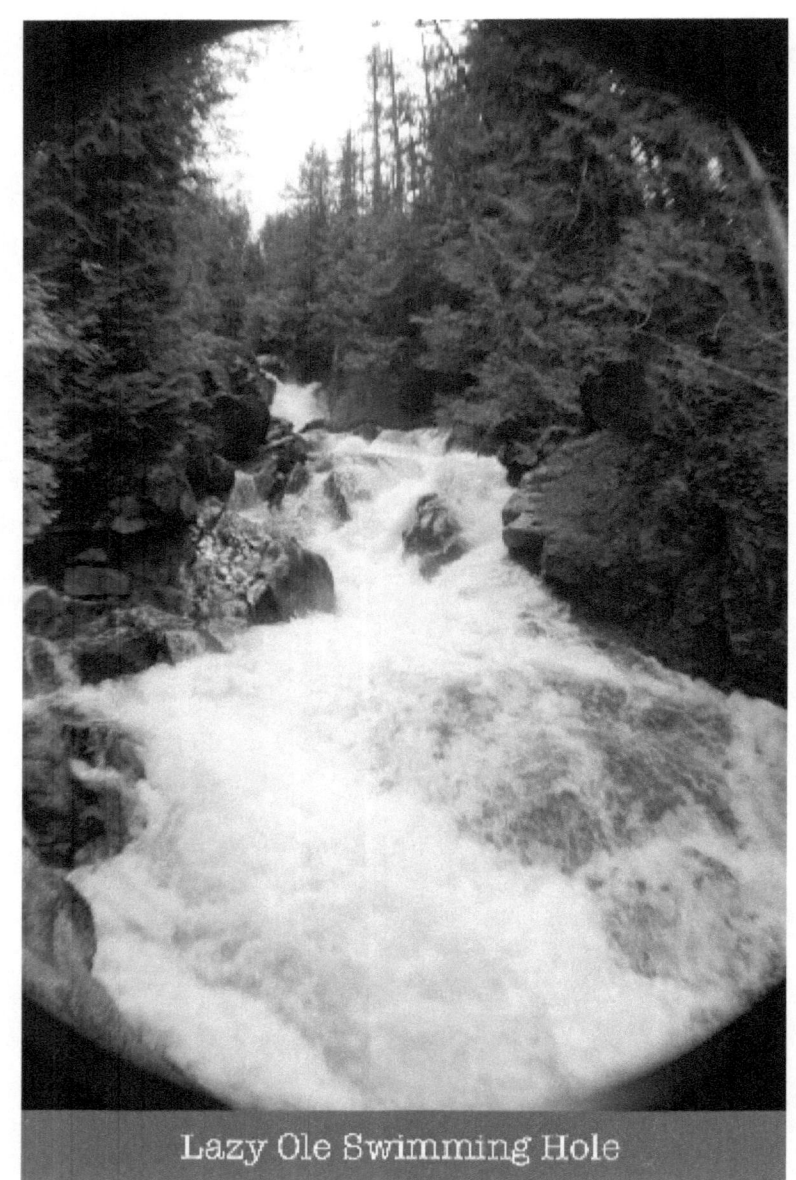
Lazy Ole Swimming Hole

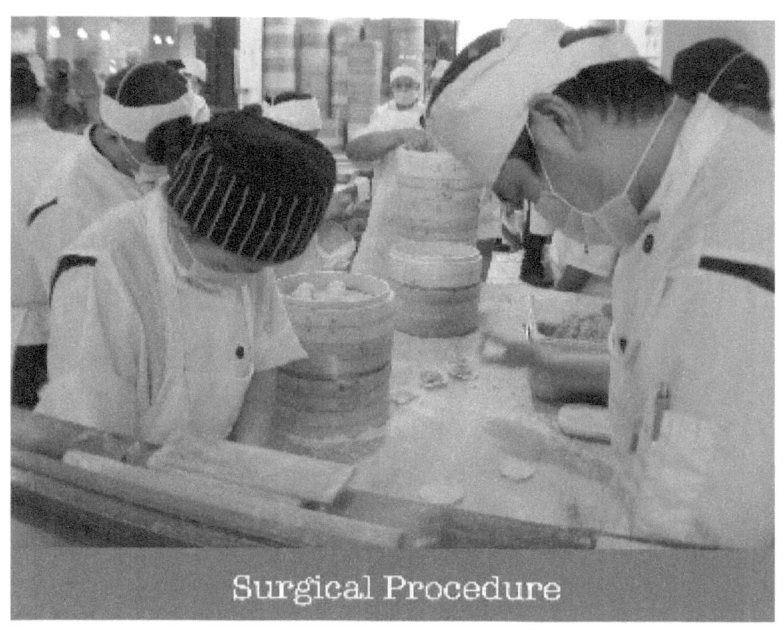
Surgical Procedure

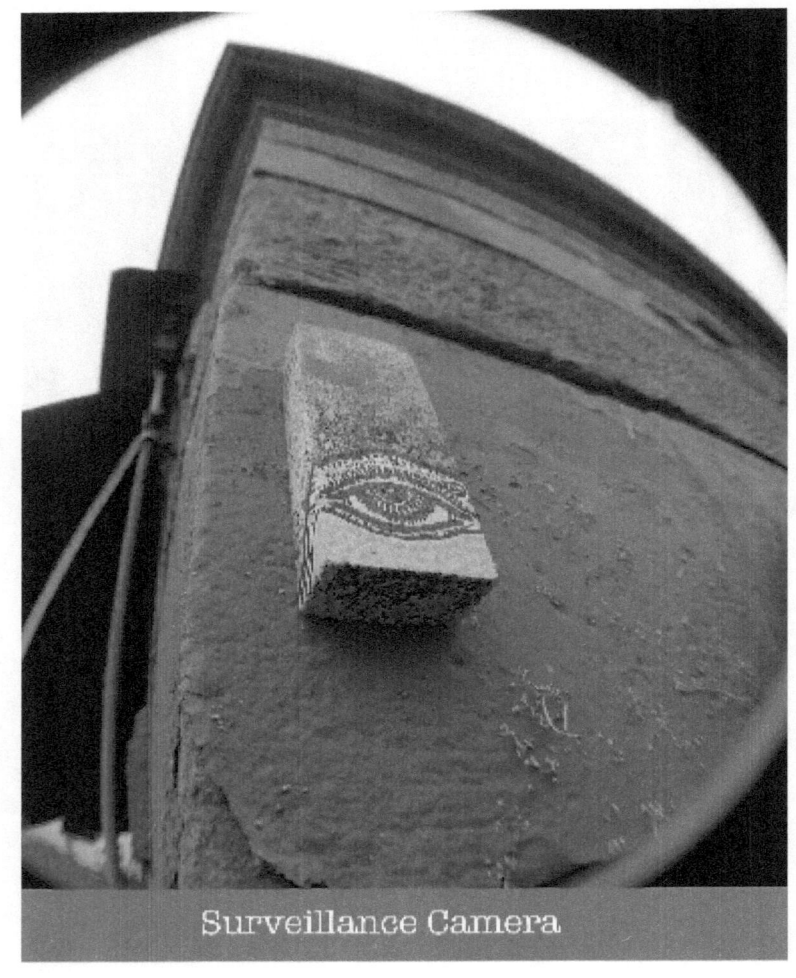

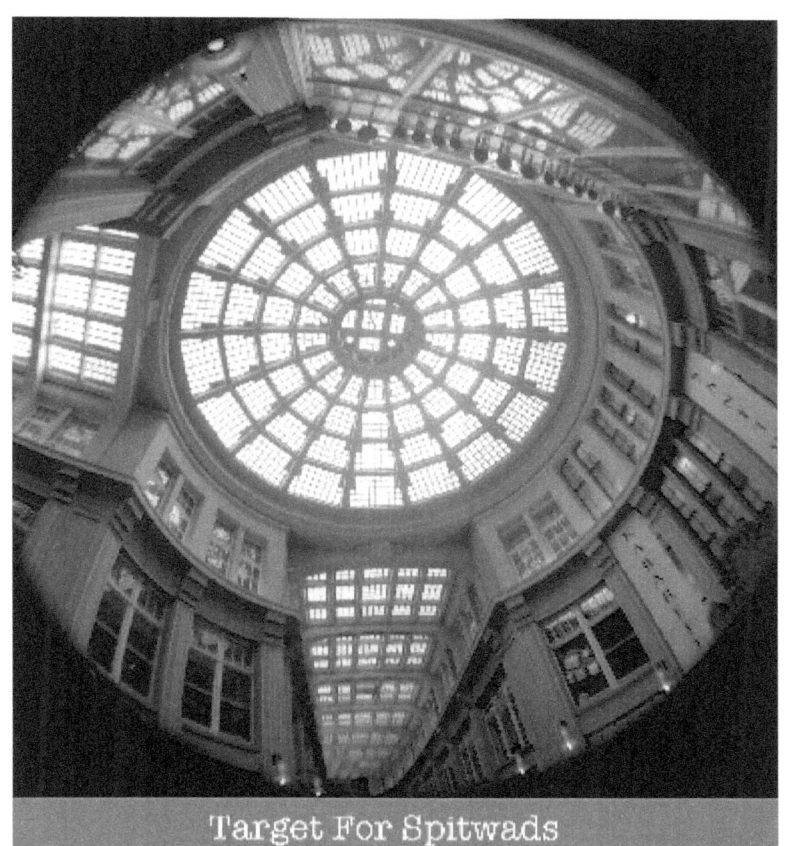

Target For Spitwads

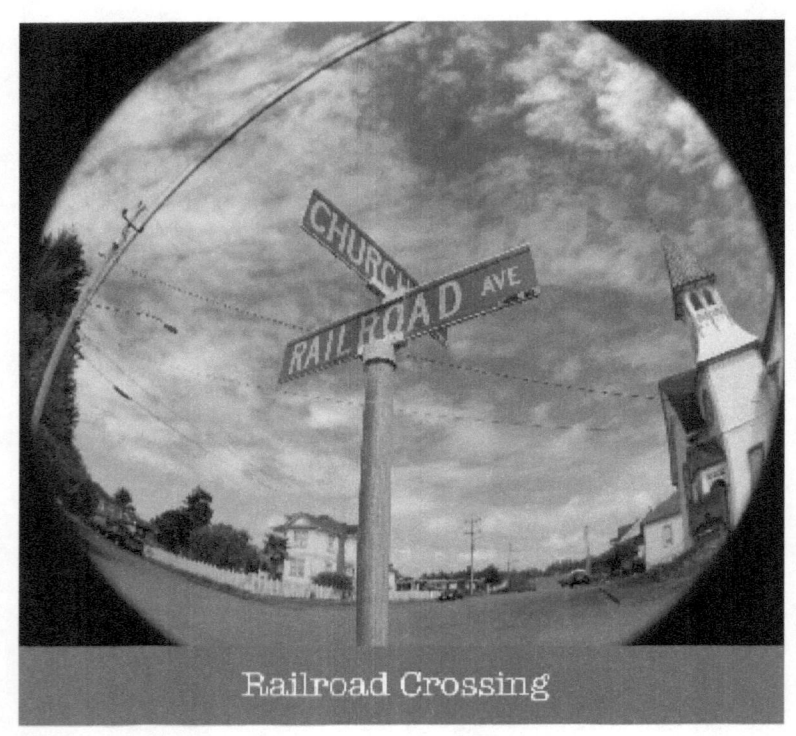

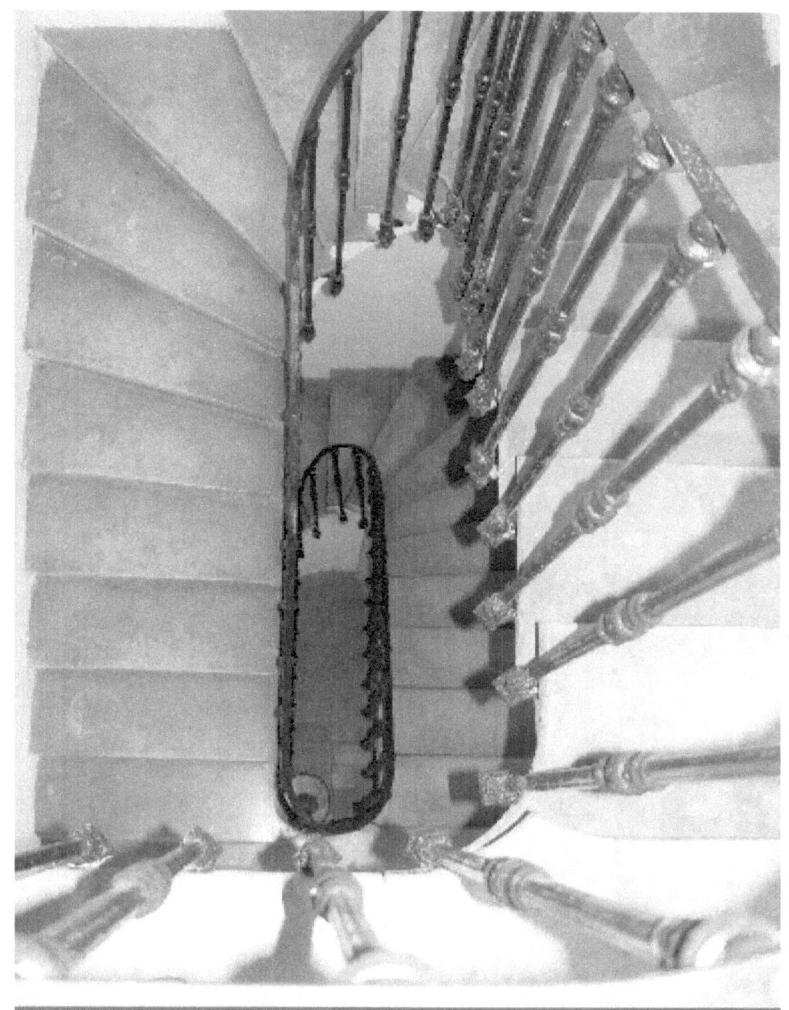

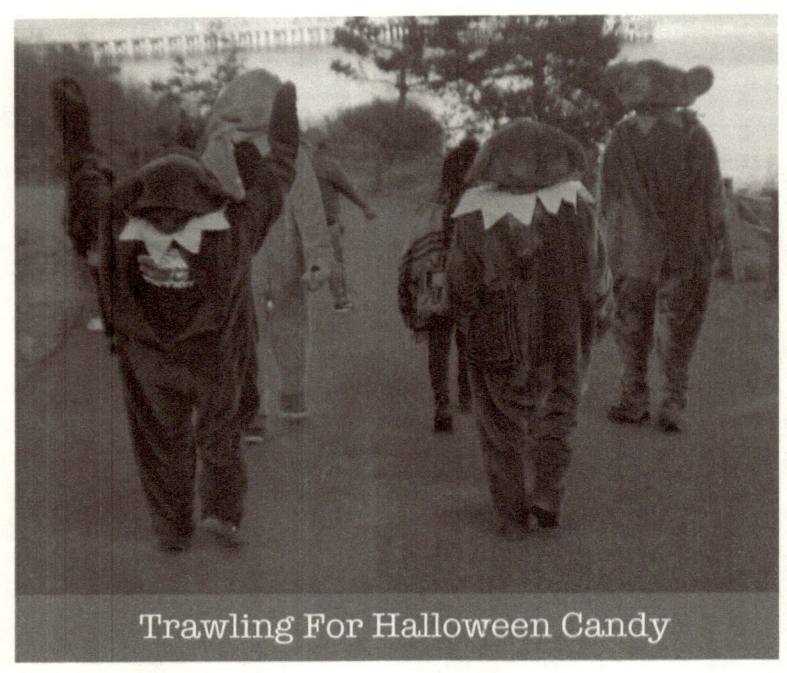
Trawling For Halloween Candy

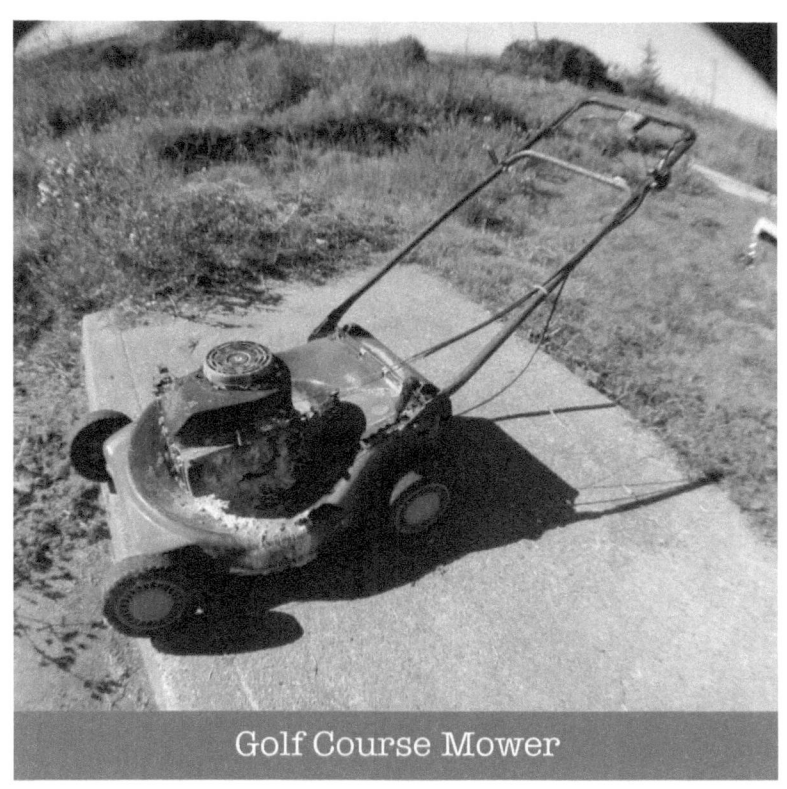
Golf Course Mower

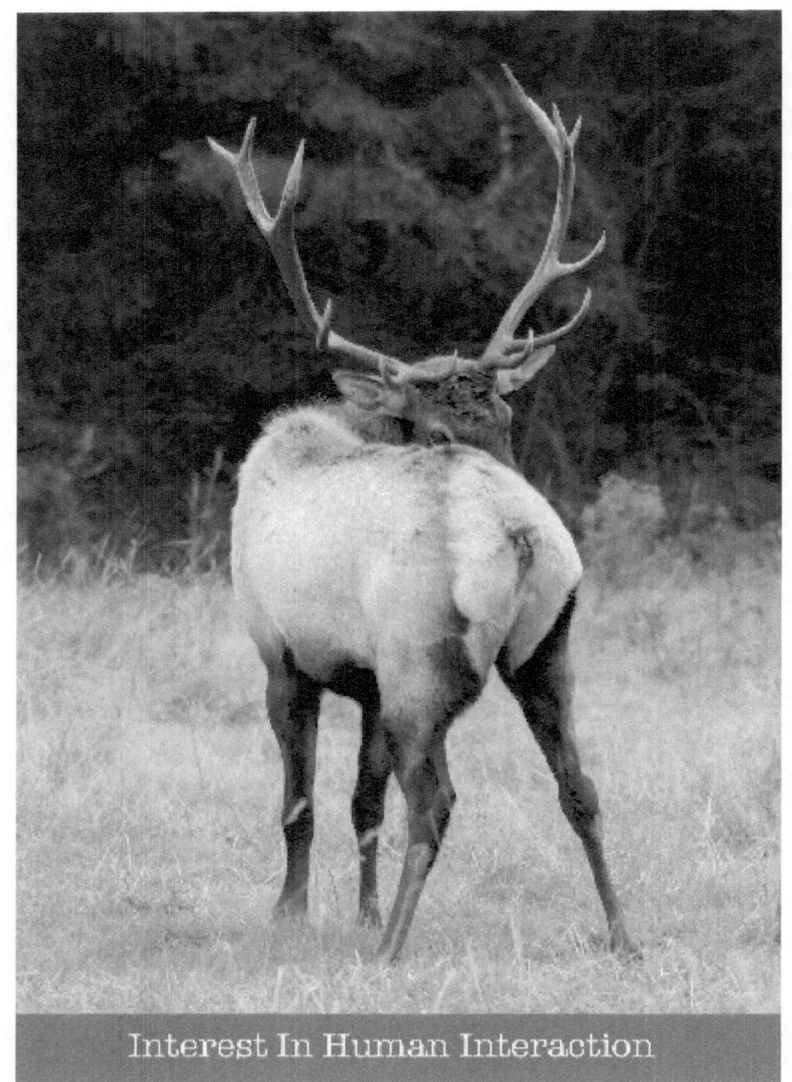
Interest In Human Interaction

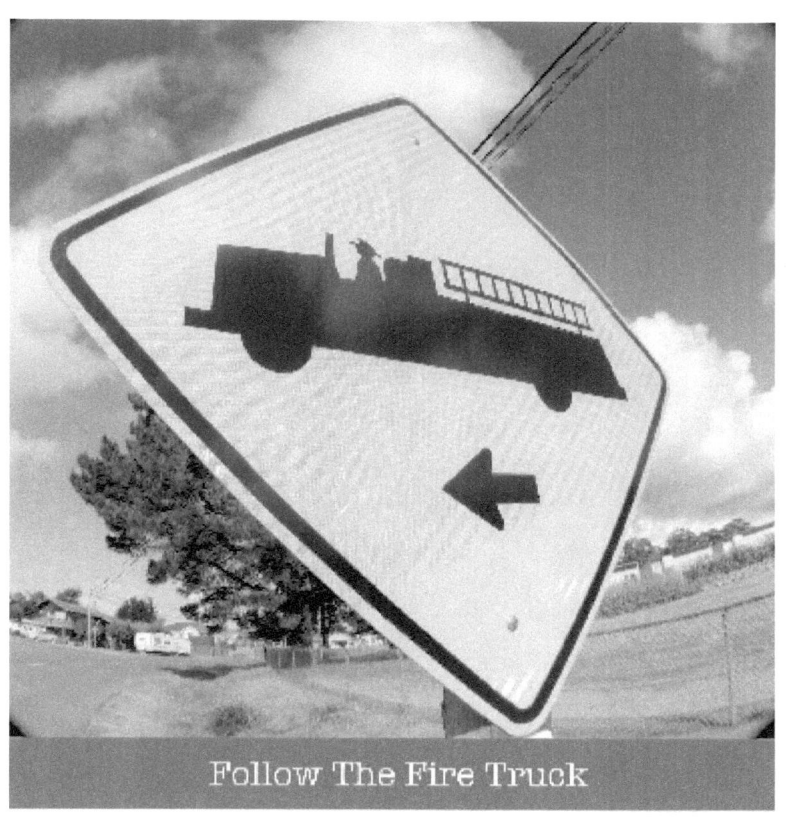

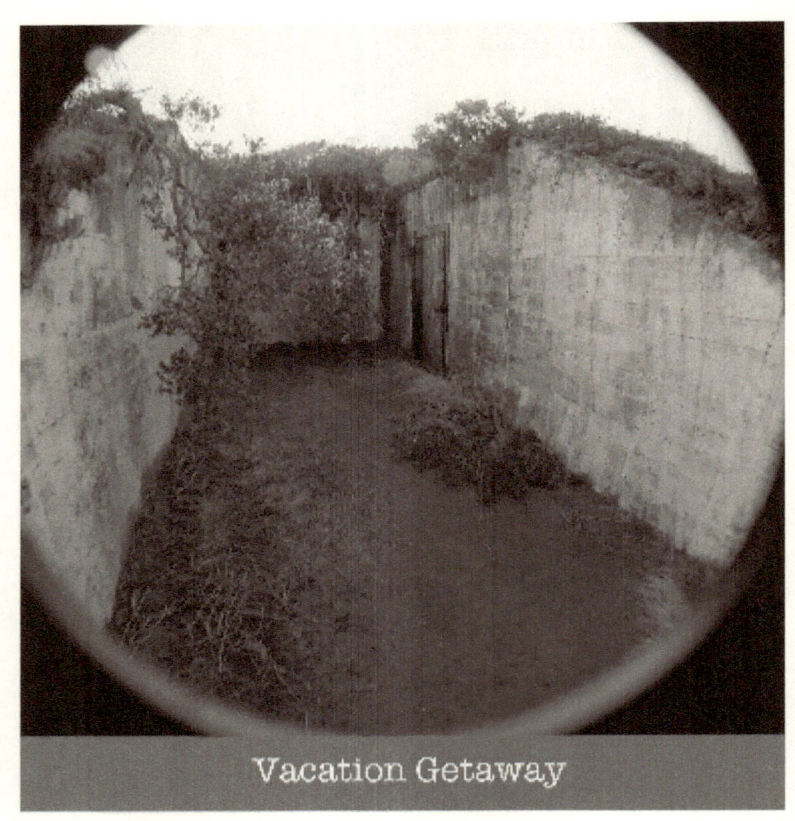
Vacation Getaway

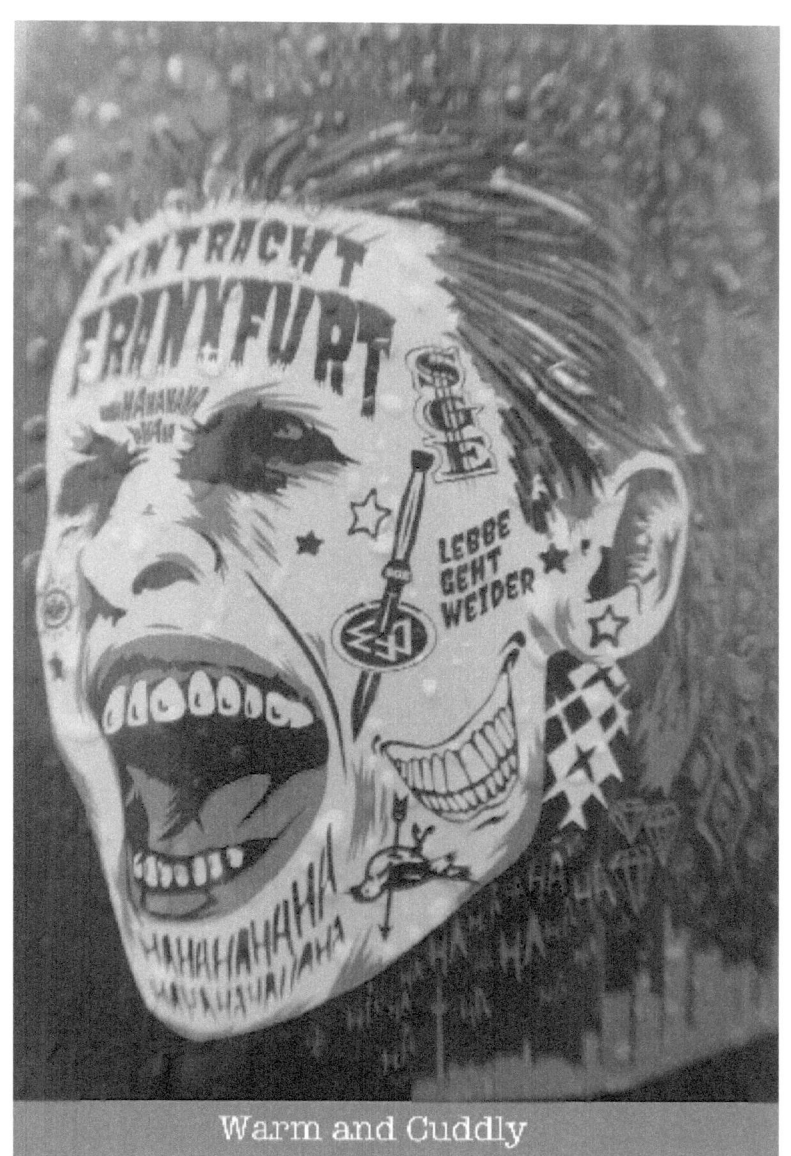

Warm and Cuddly

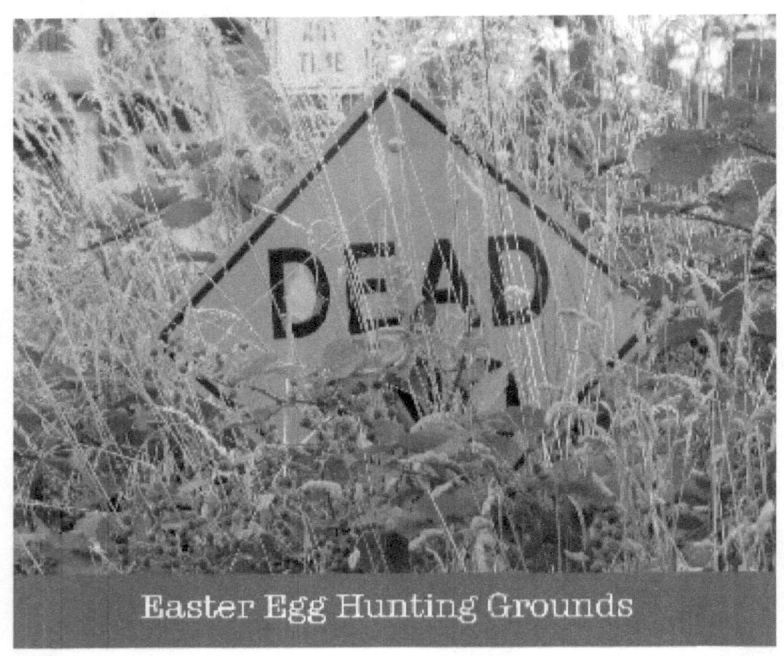

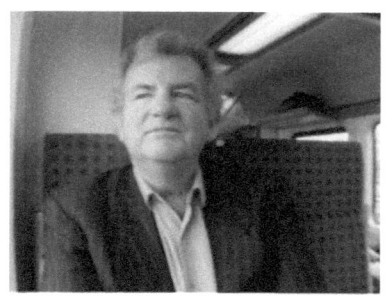

Author, photographer and visual artist Marques Vickers was born in 1957 in Vallejo, California. He graduated from Azusa Pacific University in Los Angeles and became the Public Relations and Executive Director for the Burbank, California Chamber of Commerce between 1979-84.

Professionally, he has operated travel, apparel, wine, rare book and publishing businesses. His paintings and sculptures have been exhibited in art galleries, private collections and museums in the United States and Europe. He has previously lived in the Burgundy and Languedoc regions of France and currently lives in the South Puget Sound region of Western Washington.

He has written and published over one hundred books spanning a diverse variety of subjects including true crime, international travel, social satire, wine production, architecture, history, fiction, auctions, fine art, poetry and photojournalism.

He has two daughters, Charline and Caroline who reside in Europe.

www.ingramcontent.com/pod-product-compliance
Lightning Source LLC
Chambersburg PA
CBHW020443220526
45464CB00002B/842